JOURNAL

OF AN

AVATAR

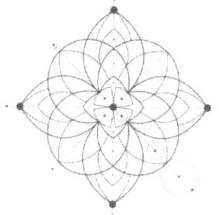

DAVID SPANGLER

Endorsements

"David Spangler offers some wonderful metaphors, recollections and insights about integrating the soul's journey with the ups and downs of day to day life. He highlights the challenge of deepening our experience of Love and standing firm in the Light while while responding intelligently and with compassion to world suffering. He is deeply insightful as to the nature of consciousness and his personal way of integrating cosmic consciousness with daily life. David reminds us that the beginning, middle and end of the journey is about Love."

—**William Bloom,** author of *Psychic Protection; The Endorphin Effect* and others.

"This book is both a gentle teacher and guide, and an enlivening inspiration. In it, David offers not only an engaging story but also the means for us to come into an ever-deepening sense of presence, light, and love. It is a book to nourish and inspire the heart—to say yes to love, yes to life, yes to who we truly are.

—**Nancy J. Napier,** author of *Sacred Practices for Conscious Loving; Meditations & Rituals for Conscious Living* and others.

"Here is a unique and special book! As a fictive spiritual biography, it blends personal experience, dreams, visions, imagination and spiritual teachings into a message needed for our time. David Spangler is a true visionary and a master author, his ability to blend fiction and genuine psychic experience with humor and everydayness creates a new context for transmitting embodied esoteric teachings. It is an entertaining, imaginary, luminous, creative work filled with love, peace, humility, and joy! Happy reading!"

—**Lee Irwin, PhD,** is the author of many books and articles on spirituality, including more recently, *Dreams Beyond Time: On Sacred Encounter and Spiritual Transformation; Sophos Ontology: On Post-Traditional Spirituality;* and *Divine Feminine Gnosis: The Lesser and Greater Mysteries of Sophia.*

"An extraordinary, profound and deeply moving book, which only this author could have written. Once read never forgotten."

—**John Matthews,** author of numerous books including *Temples of the Grail* and *The Great Book of King Arthur.*

Journal of an Avatar

Edited by Julia, Nadia and Maryn Spangler

Cover Design by Asha Hossain Design LLC

Published by Lorian Press LLC
Coloma, Michigan

ISBN: 978-1-939790-72-9

Spangler/David
Journal of an Avatar/David Spangler

First Print Edition: January 2025

Printed in the United States of America
and other countries

www.lorian.org

October, 2024

Acknowledgements

This book began as a suggestion given one night by my subtle colleagues, the friends with whom I work in the non-physical realms. I have felt their loving inspiration and support throughout the writing process, and it has been a joy for which I am deeply grateful.

I am also grateful for the invaluable help given by my family. My wife, Julia, and my daughters, Maryn and Nadia, all offered both creative suggestions and editing. Elaine Orland and Timothy Hass also had editing suggestions. Taken together, these have all made this book better than it would have been.

I am further grateful for the work done by my friend and publisher, Jeremy Berg, and for the wonderful art and design given by Asha Hossain.

The love and support of all these people enable this book to emerge as a gift of love. Thank you to each and all of you.

David Spangler

Avatar (from the Sanskrit noun avatāra) means descent, alight, to make one's appearance and refers to the embodiment of the essence of a superhuman being or a deity in human form. The Sacred becoming a person and taking on flesh.

Today I discovered I'm an avatar.

An avatar? A divine incarnation?

I know, I know...pretty incredible, right? I'm still trying to understand what it means.

It will certainly come as a surprise to my wife!

The knowledge didn't come with bells and whistles, let me tell you; no trumpets sounded. The heavens didn't open nor did a host of angels descend upon me.

It was a quiet affair.

Oh, well, there *was* one angel.

How did it happen?

I was sitting in my favorite coffee shop, contemplating my cup of coffee. The barista had made a funny little pattern in the foam on top. It wasn't really a picture of anything, just some clever swirls, light against dark, but it captivated my attention.

My mind went blank.

And I remembered.

I remembered who I was.

I remembered saying yes to this assignment.

Yes to being an avatar.

That's when the angel appeared, looking all normal in a bright, Monday-morning way in a light gold business suit, sitting down at the table across from me. He didn't have wings or a halo or anything like that, but I knew right away who...and what...he was. Perhaps it was something in his eyes. Or his smile.

Or the faint Light around him and the aura of freshness as if he'd just had the best shower in the world.

"You've remembered," he said, and those were his

first words.

"Yes," I replied. What else could I say? I really did remember.

"I wondered if you would, if today might be the day."

I shrugged. "It must have been the coffee," I said, trying to make light of the matter while my mind struggled to understand the implications. I mean, I *knew*, but I was having trouble accepting it all…what had just happened, the memories, and the angel.

"Yes," he said, smiling, going along with me. "A Premium brand, no doubt."

"I'm an avatar!" I whispered to him.

"Yes."

"Sacredness incarnate."

"Yes."

"And you're an angel!"

"Yes. Your guardian angel."

"And we're sitting here in a coffee shop!"

He looked around as if to confirm my observation. "Yes."

"But it's so…so ordinary!"

He smiled again. "Yes. Isn't it wonderful?"

"But…but why haven't I known this all along? I'm 60 years old! How come I just remembered? You'd think being an avatar isn't something I'd forget!"

"Unless you had a reason to."

"What reason would that be?"

The angel shrugged. "I don't know. You're the avatar."

"So, now what happens? What am I supposed to do?"

"That's up to you."

"Me?"

"Yes. As I said, you're the avatar."

I didn't know what to say. I was, as they say, non-plussed. Gobsmacked. Shell-shocked.

"I do have one suggestion. Start a journal."

"A journal?"

"Yes. Keep a record of what happens to you, of your thoughts and your feelings as you go along and things develop."

"As things develop? What things?"

"Never mind for now. Just keep a journal and put down your thoughts. We'll talk more when you've had a chance to adjust. Just take it easy for a day or so. Get used to the idea. The world won't end in the meantime."

And like that, he wasn't sitting across the table from me anymore.

He just vanished.

No one in the coffee shop seemed to have noticed.

So, there I was, coffee cup on the table before me, as if nothing had changed.

But everything had changed.

I remembered. I knew. And my whole world had shifted.

I did the only thing I could do.

I drank my coffee.

And started this journal.

I said that I remembered saying "yes" to being an avatar. But who did I say "yes" to?

Was it God?

An angel?

My soul?

All of the above?

The vexing thing is that I don't know. The "Yes" was implicit in the remembrance. It's not that I had no choice; we always have choice. It's that "yes" was what I chose.

But when did this happen?

It's not as if I remember a meeting in which someone said, "Would you like to be an avatar?" I would love it if there were such a memory. I would have someone to thank in moments of wonder and delight when all is going well. I would have someone to blame when it all goes pear-shaped.

Perhaps there is no "who."

Perhaps I just said "yes" to love.

Let me tell you what happened this morning.

I went into the bathroom as usual, and I picked up my electric shaver. But before I could start shaving, before I even turned it on, I felt its life in my hand. How do I explain this? There it was, an electric rotary shaver, the same shaver I used every morning, but today, it wasn't just a shaver. It was a tiny point of life, a little bit of God shaped like a shaver.

I could feel it in my hand like a tiny bird, life pulsing within it as if it had a heart. As if in response, I felt my own heart open and a wave of love come pouring out from me to it, thanking and blessing it.

It loved me back!

I felt it, flowing from the shaver into my hand and up my arm: a tingle of love.

I forgot about shaving. Instead, I put the shaver down and looked at the other things in my bathroom. There was my toothbrush (I think it's time for a new one, journal), and a crumpled tube of toothpaste. There was a plastic cup. There was a comb and a brush. And every one of them was alive.

No, they didn't sprout eyes and look at me, nor did they jump up and run around. But they were shimmering with an energy of life. The Sacred was in each of them, and all I could feel was love for them and gladness we were together and delight at being part of a world so filled with life,

I laughed out loud for the sheer joy of it.

My wife, who was still lying in bed, asked me what was so funny, and I said, "Everything!"

I was smiling as I shaved, and my shaver was smiling, too. So was my toothbrush and my comb. I could feel them.

I was in a bathroom filled with smiles.

What a nice way to start the day!

"You're high on something," my wife said today. "Do you have new meds?"

"It's just life," I said. "I've been feeling in love with everything!"

"Well, she replied, "that's great! You can love everything as long as it's not young and pretty."

Of course, she was just kidding. She has always been, is now, and will always be the one woman for me. She is my goddess, my beloved, and my partner.

But I confess, I'm at a loss as to how to tell her I'm now an avatar.

And that I'm in love with the world!

After three days of smiling, the feelings of joy and love are becoming more manageable. Instead of grinning and laughing with everything, which both delighted and concerned my wife, I feel more subdued, more in control. I still feel the love, but it's shifted to a quieter, more stable place within me.

Does this make sense?

The angel appeared again today, dressed like before, golden suit and all.

"How are you feeling?" he asked.

"Better," I replied. "I still feel in love with everything, but it's not so...overwhelming."

"Good. You're stabilizing."

"But I still don't know what I'm supposed to be doing. What does an avatar do? Preach to the masses? Heal the sick? Raise the dead? Redeem the world?"

The angel laughed. "I think that's been done. The question is, what do *you* want to do?"

"How would I know? I've never been an avatar before! Don't you have a manual for me?"

"You *are* the manual," he said, touching me on the chest.

That's when the memory came. Don't ask me from where. Presumably the same place as the memory of being an avatar. I saw and heard one of my predecessors say, "I am the Way," and I knew that statement was not meant the way it sounded...or the way it was translated. Those who heard him and those who followed after put the emphasis on the wrong place. They emphasized the "Way," and used it to mean a dogma, a belief or practice that needed to be followed. Like the path on a map.

Lots of troubles ensued from that, especially if you followed a different way.

Or had a different map.

In this memory, I could see that my predecessor meant that who he was—his way of living life—shaped the way he moved forward, day by day. It determined what he did. The emphasis should have been on the "I am."

It's as if he were saying, "Be like I *am*, don't just copy what I *do*."

I guess I am *my* Way.

And not just me! Whoever we are, we create our lives out of ourselves, hopefully out of who we are as our sacred selves.

Who else can we be and still bring the Light of our being into the world from where we may have hidden it?

We are each a sacred Way.

I'm frightened by what happened today.

I think I had a glimpse of what being an avatar could mean....and it makes me wish I'd read the fine print before I said yes.

I watched horrible news on the television. There was another mass shooting, this time in a school, and several children had died, along with their teacher. The shooter took his own life.

All at once, the grief, the pain, the fear, the anger, the hatred and despair caused by this event rose up before me like some miasmic cloud of darkness. It hovered there in the air before me, and I knew that I was supposed to step into it and bring healing and Light.

I couldn't do it.

I was afraid I'd be lost within it.

Who could take on such suffering and survive?

An avatar could.

Perhaps an avatar should.

But I couldn't.

I stepped back, and the cloud disappeared.

I feel like I failed.

All the love and joy I've been feeling...surely there was a power there that I could have used, that could have been healing. But to step into and take on such darkness...

I don't know. Is this what an avatar does?

I don't think I can.

The angel came again today.

I was feeling depressed after my experience—my failure—two days ago. I was angry at myself and confused. I couldn't write anything yesterday.

I asked for help, and the angel came, golden suit, smiles, and all.

"I failed yesterday," I said.

"No," he said, "you didn't fail. You simply said no to an experience that felt threatening and overwhelming."

"But…" His remark confused me even more. I had been expecting him to agree with me. "But…wasn't it a test?"

"A test? What kind of test?"

"A test of me being an avatar, of course, and being able to help people in need. Of confronting darkness! A test I failed!"

"There was no test. You don't need to prove to us that you're an avatar. We can see that you are."

"But…"

The angel held up his hand to stop me. "There was no test. Your heart has been open to love and to the Light and joy within creation. Correct?"

I nodded.

"Then you encountered a tragedy, and your openness put you in touch with all the tragedies that humanity has experienced. Thousands…no, hundreds of thousands of years of trauma. A scream within the unconscious mind of humanity." The angel sighed. "We deal with this every day. It's more than any one human, even an avatar, can handle on their own. Only God is big enough, loving enough, inclusive enough, healing enough to transmute all that darkness. And," he held up his hand to stop me from interrupting him, "it would be transmuted, except that human beings find excuses to hold onto their trauma." He sighed again. "You find hiding within the shadows of your pain safer than accepting your sacredness and standing in your Light."

It was the most the angel had said to me.

"Each of you," he continued, reaching out to touch my chest, "can bring Light into this darkness, a little bit at a time. You don't have to be an avatar to do that, but you do have to trust the Light within you, and the love."

"I didn't trust myself."

"You were caught by surprise. Get over it. Next time you'll do better."

"Next time....?"

"What? You thought human suffering disappeared overnight? You acted wisely in that moment by saying no. Taking on more than you can handle will only add to the problem...which, frankly, you are doing now by feeling sorry for yourself. So, be an avatar and stop it!"

With that he disappeared, leaving me still confused, but, I admit, feeling better about the experience.

I guess being an avatar means learning on the job...

I saved a life today.

And I learned a lesson.

I was out for a morning walk when I came across a large earthworm crawling slowly across the sidewalk. It had rained during the night, so there was a little moisture on the concrete, but the sun was out. I knew the pavement would dry up quickly, and, unless it reached the other side and could burrow into the moist soil, so would the earthworm.

I couldn't let that happen. I reached down and picked the worm up, feeling its moist body squirm and contract in my hand. I carried it over to a nearby bush and put it on the ground in the shade. It lay there for a moment, then I felt a wave of love from it to me, and I swear that it said "Thank you," though not in words. It then burrowed into the soil.

Then, it was as if I became that earthworm, eating its way through the earth, creating little tunnels that aerated the soil, allowing air and moisture to penetrate the dark places. I saw myself breaking up the hard, dry earth, turning it into rich nurturing soil from which life could spring.

Coming back to my human self, I realized what I was being shown.

To be an avatar is to be an earthworm.

When I had faced the hard, fearful darkness of human suffering, I could have been the earthworm that burrowed in and transmuted that darkness into Light and new life. I was frightened because I thought I had to deal with the whole thing, but the earthworm isn't trying to eat all the earth, only the little bit right in front of it. And it eats what it can digest and transform.

Now I know.

Next time, I will burrow fearlessly, "eating" just what the love within me can digest and transmute.

A life was helped today. The question is, was it the earthworm's…or was it mine?

We helped each other.

We were each other's avatar.

Today, I discovered the Lineage.

It turns out there are a bunch of us….avatars, I mean.

Or there have been.

Or will be.

It's a little confusing as the Lineage exists outside of time, so it is of the past, but it's also of the present and, I guess, of the future.

I haven't quite figured all of that out.

I was in my study preparing for my day's work on my latest fantasy novel. All at once, I found myself surrounded by a crowd of people. Transparent people, like ghosts, or people made of smoke or light. My study was filled with them, men and women.

They were all just standing there, mingling, as if it were a cocktail party of some kind, though no one had a drink in their hand. They were talking with each other, but I couldn't hear them. For me, the room was silent. Yet, I felt as if I knew each of them. They were all familiar, like being in a family gathering. We were kin, in some way.

Then I saw the angel. This time, he wasn't dressed in a suit but was robed in Light. No, it was as if his body and clothes were all one thing and that was Light.

He came up to me, gestured at the crowd, and said, "This is your Lineage."

"My what?" I asked.

"Those like you. Your Lineage. Avatars. Those who have been, are now, and will be avatars."

"I'm part of a Lineage? You mean, there are more like me?"

The angel smiled. "Of course. You're not alone."

I looked around at all the figures, none of whom seemed to notice me. "Can they see me? Can I talk to them?"

The angel shook his head. "Not yet. But soon. First, there will be memories."

"Memories?"

He smiled again. "Yes. One at a time. Soon."

Then he and the group disappeared, and I was alone in my study, feeling a little like Ebeneezer Scrooge when he was told he'd be visited by three spirits. "One at a time? Can't I take them all at once?"

Apparently not.

There's more to this avatar gig than I thought.

I wonder what I'll remember first?

Today, my wife said to me, "Are you an avatar?"

"Who told you that?" I asked.

"I had a dream. An angel told me. This is why you've been grinning so much."

My wife is a prolific dreamer. Occasionally, her dreams are prophetic, as when she dreamt after we first met that we would get married.

"An angel told you…in a dream?"

"Yes. He said you were now an avatar and that it was best that I knew this so that I would understand if you did strange things."

"What strange things?"

"He didn't say, but I told him you were always doing strange things, so how would I tell the difference?" She smiled with the memory. "He laughed. Did you know angels laugh? Doesn't matter. *Are* you an avatar?"

"Apparently," and I told her about my experience in the coffee shop and meeting the angel. "But I still don't know what to do or what it means."

She shrugged and gave me a hug. "I guess we'll find out. Just don't do anything too strange!"

I've not felt like writing anything for a couple of days. Life is normal.

I thought after the angel told my wife I was an avatar that there might be a little more reverence around the house...nothing extravagant, you understand, but maybe an occasional genuflection or "your holiness" directed my way.

Not from my wife! She treats me as she always has, with love and tolerance and more than a bit of humor. If there were any danger of my avatarness giving me a swelled head, she would be the first to shrink it back down to size.

Which is likely why the angel told her.

Not that I *was* getting a swelled head, you understand....

The first memory came today, and it was a doozy.

It was of one of my predecessors in the Lineage, the one I'd always thought of as *The* Avatar, the Christ.

In my memory, he was sitting alone on a rock atop a small rise, apparently lost in thought. I must have had a question because I was climbing up to him. The ground was rocky and barren, and I had to be careful with my footing.

His head was bowed when I came up to him, but he raised his face to me. He didn't resemble the pictures people paint of him now, with long hair and beard. His hair was short, as was his beard, and there was a youthfulness about him that spoke of vitality and strength. But it was his eyes….

I will never forget his eyes.

He looked at me, and there was such a depth of love and sadness in his eyes, as well as a sense of wonder. It was as if everything he saw was filled with the Light of God, which constantly amazed and delighted him. Yet, at the same time, he could see what was ahead, how the Light in us would be denied, hence the sadness.

And there was something more. In his eyes, I saw my own fate. I saw that one day, I would be where he was, sharing his burden, seeing with his eyes, and it frightened me. He was an elder brother who had traveled the road he knew I would travel and knew what it meant and what was ahead.

It was a vision of the future I didn't want to have at that moment, and he knew that. And this went into his love and his sadness, too. He didn't speak, but it was as if he had said, "You follow my road, for which I am glad, but it will not be easy to share my burden."

That was the memory.

He knew that one day I would be an avatar, and it both gladdened and saddened his heart. In that moment, I wanted nothing more than to hug him, protect him, and comfort him, and let him know his path was not a burden but an act of love I was privileged to share.

Later, my wife found me crying in our bedroom.

"One of those strange things?" she asked.

I nodded.

She came over and just wrapped her arms around me and held me as a lover holds her beloved, or a mother holds her child.

I'm so glad the angel told her what I was.

After a quiet day yesterday, in which I tried to digest what I had remembered, more memories came today.

They were not as focused as the first one. They were more of a collage of images as I saw myself following my Predecessor around as he taught and as he healed.

Teaching and healing....not in my skill set. At least not yet.

In these memories, I saw not only what was happening in the physical world but in a subtler reality as well. As Jesus lived his life and performed, not just his miracles but his everyday, ordinary activities and encounters, his energy entered into the aura of people, triggering a shift of consciousness. They were ordinary people who found their lives and their energy fundamentally changed. The relationship between their souls and their physical identities was shifted. They saw in Jesus their own sacredness reflected back to them in the mirror of ordinary life. They began to say yes to love and yes to life.

This was not the spreading of a doctrine that eventually morphed into a church but the spreading of a soul capacity, an incarnational capacity to embody love, and it did so through ordinary people doing ordinary things.

Maybe I don't have to know how to heal or how to raise the dead or walk on water or perform miracles to be an avatar.

Maybe I just need to be who I am, be an example of saying yes to love.

Date ~ August 11

I'm trying to be better about writing to you every day, which is hard when you have days like today when nothing really happens. But I guess a break is OK, every now and then.

I can't expect every day to be filled with revelations!

I feel like I'm being trained, that my desire to know how to be an avatar and what I should be doing is being answered. But never directly. I have to discern the lesson.

Case in point: the angel appeared and suggested I attend a spiritual conference being held in the city near where I live. Normally, I would avoid such an affair. I don't like being in crowds of people, for one thing. But an angelic suggestion is, well, an angelic suggestion, and though I knew I could say no, I saw no real reason to object.

So, off I went to the conference.

When I say "conference," it was more like a street fair inside a hotel. Numerous occult, metaphysical, and spiritual groups had set up booths and were competing for attention. There was music, and there was dancing, and smaller lecture rooms were set aside to accommodate a schedule of presentations that would have choked a mule. I think there were three lectures or workshops scheduled for every hour: a veritable smorgasbord of teachings whose main effect seemed to be producing a growing cadre of glassy-eyed, exhausted attendees wiped out by the competing choices.

Not my usual cup of tea!

On the other hand, this seemed like it could be prime territory for expressing my avatarness if I just knew how to let people know I was there.

Except someone else beat me to it.

There was a lavish booth, garish to my eyes but then again, no more so than some of its neighbors. It proclaimed in glittering letters that here was the Messiah, the Promised One, the Avatar of the Age.

I decided to check it out. Was this a colleague or competition?

The booth was manned by tanned, handsome and beautiful young men and women, all wearing white tunics and trousers. They looked like they were advertisements for a fitness spa, but instead, they were handing out leaflets or selling merchandise with distinctly occult flavors, sincerely proclaiming that their Master was The One.

There was a commotion, and the crowd around the booth parted as a phalanx of muscled young men moved people to one side, not always too gently, proclaiming that "the Master is here." And sure enough, in the middle of these muscular disciples was a man who looked like he'd been picked from central casting for the role of avatar. A well-trimmed beard under an eagle's nose, long, flowing locks, a pure white robe, black eyes glittering with suppressed power...charisma and energy flowed off him like water off the falls at Niagara.

He and his entourage walked quickly as if headed into their booth, but suddenly, he swerved and changed direction, creating some confusion among the ranks of his bodyguards who quickly had to reform around him. To my surprise and, I admit, consternation, this apparition of Messiah-hood strode over and stopped right in front of me.

He grabbed my shoulders with both hands and pulled me into a quick hug. Then, releasing me but with his eyes boring into mine, he said, "I am the Master."

"Glad to meet you," I said. "I'm an avatar too!"

In that moment, I saw past all the energy, all the charisma, all the facade he had built up around himself and with which he charmed and controlled his followers. What I saw was a small, frightened soul, caught up in more than it could handle, riding a tiger of other people's expectations and wanting to get off before it turned on him with its claws and teeth. It looked at me and mouthed the words, "Help me!"

"I love you," I said out loud. "Just say yes to love and free yourself." And I felt a wave of love flow out from me to the soul within the "Master."

For a moment, I thought he might respond. But then the Master jerked back. "Screw you!" he snarled, and turned and went back towards his booth, his bodyguards glaring at me as they followed.

At that point, I left the conference and went home. There was nothing there for me.

After I got home from the spiritual conference yesterday, the angel appeared to me. He was back to wearing his golden suit. "Well," he said, "we rolled the dice, but it didn't work out, did it?"

"You mean with the Master?"

"Yes. There was a chance to free him. He's not a bad sort. He's just caught up in something he doesn't understand that's larger than he is."

"I saw his soul. He looked frightened."

"As well he should be. It's no small thing to take on the thought-form of a Messiah or an Avatar. People have expectations, and if you can't fulfill them…" the angel drew a finger across his throat in a gesture that needed no elaboration.

We were in my study, and I sat down in a chair. The angel sat on the sofa opposite me. "This was a lesson for me, wasn't it?" I said.

The angel grinned. "Oh, did you learn something?"

I grinned back. "I learned that if I want to be a proper avatar, I need followers, disciples, oh, and pamphlets and maybe some merchandise. An avatar coffee mug, maybe."

"And a white robe."

"Oh, definitely a white robe!"

We both laughed.

"It's funny, yes," the angel said. "To me, all human activity has a funny side. But it's tragic, as well. The Master will not come to a happy end in this life. But his soul will learn and eventually, who knows, he may truly become a master."

"I hope so," I replied. "But coming back to me, yes,

I learned that self-promotion is not the way to go. Not," I added quickly, "that I was intending to go that way!"

"I didn't think you were. But you do keep asking, what should I do? What does an avatar do? I thought maybe an example of what not to do would be instructive."

And with that thought in the air, he disappeared.

But then I heard his voice, saying, "Don't overthink it. You'll figure it out. It's what you told the Master. Just say yes to love."

Then silence truly descended upon the room.

Date ~ August 14

I've been thinking about my encounter with the "Master" since it happened. He seemed to think that being an avatar meant having to be perfect. Many people seem to share that expectation, that an avatar is a summit of spiritual perfection and power, but I don't believe it's true. Something in my memory or my intuition tells me otherwise.

I think people get it the wrong way around. The mountain peak may be a place of purity, beauty, and vista, but it's in the messiness of the valley that life unfolds. That is where the fecundity is, where growth happens, where emergence pokes its novel face from behind the bushes. The valley is the happening place.

An avatar is a servant of the sacredness within all things. His or her job is to tend the life in the valley, to enable it to have even more life, more vitality, more freedom, more joy.

The mountaintop is there to serve the valley.

My son came over today to visit. His wife was working, so he brought his four-year old daughter with him. My wife and I feel blessed because he, as well as our own daughter and her husband and son, live nearby, so we get to see them often. Lots of babysitting time with grandchildren, which especially pleases my wife. Doesn't make me sorry, either.

Anyway, while my wife and granddaughter went off to a nearby park in our neighborhood to play on the swings, my son and I had a chat. He's a psychiatrist with a specialty in neuro-divergence—how our brains are all different and the implications of that in human relations. I've picked his brain a number of times for ideas for some of my novels, and I always enjoy the stimulation of our conversations.

This time, our conversation started off when my son said, "By the way, Dad, I have a cool avatar!"

I should explain that my son and I have several common interests besides brain differences. We both enjoy playing role-playing games online and on our tabletops with friends. For both of us, it's a professional interest as well as a fun hobby. In my field, I find some of the best fantasy and science fiction stories being told are through the medium of computer role playing games or CRPGs. My son in turn uses role-playing games as therapeutic tools in his counseling work with teenagers.

"Avatar?" I repeated, taken by surprise. Had the angel visited him in a dream, too?

"Yes. You know, the character that represents me in a game. It's a new game I've been trying out with some of my kids…my patients. I'm a zombie shaman healer, basically a good guy who can't be killed because I'm already dead! He's got quite a backstory."

"I'll bet," I replied, trying to wrap my mind around a zombie healer. Story possibilities were already popping up in my mind. Once a novelist…..

"The kids think he's cool, which helps my work, you know."

"I bet," I repeated, partly distracted by the story ideas. "Say," I continue, suddenly deciding to take a plunge, "I just discovered *I'm* an avatar."

"Oh? Which game are you playing now, Dad?"

"No game. In life. What do you think of that?"

He laughed. "Hell, we're all avatars here, Dad! We're all representatives of how our brains and bodies work." He reached over and squeezed my hand. "I love how your imagination works!"

And that ended our conversation on avatars.

Probably just as well. I'll wait until I perform my first miracle to bring it up again!

A red-letter day!

A member of the Lineage showed up and we had an actual conversation! I am overjoyed. I finally seem to be getting somewhere.

I was in my study, working on my latest novel, a fantasy about a haunted house. The story was falling flat, though, and I was beginning to give up hope for it when I became aware that I wasn't alone. An older woman was sitting on the sofa not far from my desk, looking at me. She was faintly transparent, not fully a ghost. There was substance there in her plain dress, but I could still make out through her the design on the Navajo blanket I have on the back of that sofa.

"Hello," I said. Having just been writing about ghosts, it somehow seemed natural that one might show up.

She patted the sofa. "Come and sit by me," she said, with no other preamble. "It will help me be more present."

I got up and walked around my desk and over to the sofa. As I got nearer to her, she did seem more and more solid until, when I sat down next to her, she was as real and physical as I was. She had on a peasant's dress, very plain, and her feet were in sandals. There was a purple ribbon in her brown hair, but otherwise, there were no other adornments. Looking at her, though, I realized she didn't need them. She had a plain face, but she radiated love. Her eyes were the same eyes I had seen in my memories of my Predecessor, windows into someplace deep and infinite and all-seeing. Luminous.

I knew immediately what she was.

Another avatar.

"My name is Lusanne," she said, "and like you, I am one of the Lineage. I, too, was an avatar. I lived a quiet life in what now is southern France. I had gifts of healing and occasionally of prophecy. Mostly, I learned to love. I did no teaching, though now and again, I shared a nugget of wisdom that I had learned. I spread light wherever I could, but I had no followers. I am not known to history. I lived a peaceful life for the most part, at least until the end."

"What happened at the end?"

"I was hung as a witch. A jealous farmer wanted my land, and I refused to sell to him." Then she smiled, and it was like sunshine suddenly filled my room. "It was my time to go. I bear no ill will."

"Were you born an avatar?" I asked, "or like me, did you suddenly find it thrust upon you?"

She shrugged. "Each of us in the Lineage has a different story. Some were born to the mission. In others, it grew like seeds until it ripened within them and revealed itself. And some became avatars because they were available, and the time demanded it." She took my hand, and I felt a thrill of energy pass through my body. "I think you are one of the latter," she said. "I was born into it."

A silence ensued as we each pursued our thoughts, then she said, "You are growing into it. I have come to reassure you. You are not alone." She released my hand. "Your time requires something different from what has gone before," she continued. "I cannot say what. None of us knows. It's an experiment."

"You mean, I'm an experiment?"

"Yes. Does this frighten you?"

I stood up, mixed emotions churning inside me, and began to pace, something I do to help me think. "I don't know. Maybe? Yes? I'm not sure? Depends on what kind of experiment."

"A good one, I assure you. One born of love. And good intentions."

"Good intentions. That's what the road to hell is paved with." I faced her. "You could be a demon in disguise!"

She laughed, and my mood, which had been turning sour, immediately lightened. "That's what the farmer said who had me hung, that I was consorting with demons!"

I grinned. "I apologize."

"No need. I guess we're all experiments in the Lineage," she said, standing up as well. "It was a burden to me, too, at first, knowing what I was but not knowing what I was to do. You, at least, are visited by an angel. I had to learn from my chickens and cows, my ducks and my sheep."

"What did you learn?" I was curious what farm animals might have taught her as an avatar.

"Why, how to say yes to love, of course, and to life."

As if that statement were some kind of celestial key which, when uttered, caused things to disappear, Lusanne faded away, though she left behind a feeling of joy in the room.

I knew I had been in the presence of a mountaintop.

Thinking about the Lineage and Lusanne, I've come to realize that avatars, like ice cream, must come in many flavors.

How could it be otherwise?

Some of us like vanilla. Some like chocolate. That fellow over there likes coffee pistachio! The Field of Love has all the flavors, so no one is left out. There's something to reach everyone.

Some avatars are like ice cream trucks, carrying a variety of flavors for many kinds of tastes. Some carry so many different flavors that we think they can feed the world. We think of them as world saviors.

Some, though, are like me: what I have is all you get. It appeals to you, or it doesn't.

If the flavor I have is the one you want, then I'm all here for you. It's yours, with my love. If it isn't, then how wonderful it is that avatars come in all possible flavors. Somewhere, somewhen, you'll find the taste you crave.

When you get down to it, though, whatever the flavor, it's still all ice cream. When it comes to avatars, it's still all love. No matter who we are, what we do, or what we bring, or how much of it, love is at the heart of it all.

It's the flavor of all flavors!

I had another memory today.

This one was fantastic. That is, it was like something out of a fantasy. Since I write fantasy stories for a living, this made me suspicious. Was this a real memory, or was it a product of my imagination? It certainly had resonances with famous fantasy tropes.

So, how to evaluate it?

I'll just have to write it down and let it sit within me.

It's a memory of an initiation. In this memory, I'm a middle-aged man with dark hair and a short black beard. There are both Muslim and Christian influences in my background, and as I concentrate on this, I feel that I am a Christian in an Islamic country, specifically Andalusia or Al-Andalus as it was known in Arabic. My sense is that it's the 11th century, and I'm living in the Almoravid Empire, a Muslim state which was centered in Morocco.

In this memory, I am in a cave high in the Atlas Mountains in Morocco. The walls of the cave are studded with large and small amethyst crystals...literally, it's a crystal cave. Torches fixed into the sides of the cave are burning, causing the crystals to glimmer and filling the cave with a purple light.

There are others in the cave with me, all members of a secret brotherhood of Light. We don't seem to have a name, so I think of them—of us—as the Amethyst Brotherhood. We are gathered to perform an initiation ritual on my behalf. It is being led by a tall man with a dark beard and luminous eyes, a white turban around his head.

In this memory, I don't recall the details of the ritual. The focus of the memory is on what happens at the moment of initiation.

In that moment, it's as if the cave becomes a single crystal with me at the center, a crystal filled with Light. A shining Presence appears before me and surrounds me with a purple light.

It says, "Do you accept this Path of Love?"

"Yes," I reply.

"Do you accept this Path of Service, whatever it calls on you to do?"

"Yes," I reply.

"Then step into a new life, one with the Lineage of Remembrance and Service."

I can feel a shift of energies within me. Something has changed. I'm no longer who I was.

Then, the Presence withdraws and disappears, and I am standing in the crystal cave, surrounded by fellow initiates.

That is the memory. I think it was the moment I became part of this Lineage.

I think it was the moment I said yes to becoming an avatar.

I spent all day yesterday thinking about my initiation in the cave. Then, today, my angel appeared again.

I was eager to tell him about my memory of the crystal cave. "This is why I'm an avatar, isn't it?" I said.

"No," he replied.

"No? But...wasn't it an initiation?"

"It's only one of many. Oh, it was dramatic, I'll grant you that, a cave of amethyst crystals and all, but really, it's all just window dressing. Theater and play, entertainment for the personality."

"Wow! You really know how to pop a balloon!"

He smiled. "I apologize. Oh, it was an important enough event in the lives of all of you who were there then. Had you been discovered, it could well have meant your deaths. But it was not what makes you an avatar. Only love can do that."

"But what about the being who came, the one who initiated me?"

"Who do you think that was? It was your soul, of course! Only you can choose to say yes to love, yes to service, yes to life."

"I made myself an avatar?"

"In a manner of speaking, yes. Who else has the power to do so? It's not a job that's assigned to you, you know."

"No, I don't know. That's just the point. I don't know. It's not like you've given me much in the way of instruction!"

"If I could, I would," he said, seriously. "Look, appreciate your crystal cave and your initiation. Just don't use it as an explanation for anything. It was an exciting moment in your soul's history. Don't read more into it than that. You're more than that moment. Don't use it as an explanation for anything or define yourself by it."

Then he disappeared.

Disappearing....best conversation stopper in the world!

Lusanne came back today.

I confess, I had been stewing over what the angel said and how to interpret the memory of the crystal cave.

As before, she appeared sitting on the sofa in my study, patting the seat beside her in an invitation to join her. Which I did.

"You've been troubled," she said.

"This whole avatar business troubles me," I said. I then shared with her my memory of the initiation in the crystal cave, what it seemed to mean, and then, what the angel had said about it. "Why have this memory," I finished, "if it's really not important and doesn't mean anything?"

She sat quietly for a time, obviously thinking. Then she said, "I have no memory like that. As far as I can tell, I never went through any initiation like you describe."

"Yet, you were an avatar."

"Yes. So, the angel must be right. It wasn't that important...or at least, not necessary. But that doesn't mean it had no value or that it wasn't a turning point for you of some nature. It was obviously a powerful experience, but it's up to you just what it means."

I sighed. "I felt it meant something...maybe a lot. Now I'm not sure."

We were both quiet after that. Finally, she said, "I'm just a plain person, not given to fancy. I just did what was in front of me and learned to say yes to love. That was all I did. Love for everything and everyone."

"Even those who killed you."

"Especially those!"

I smiled. "That was a very avatar-like thing to do."

She looked at me oddly, as if puzzled. "Was it?"

"It seems so to me."

She nodded. "Maybe so. Or maybe you need to stop trying to understand it all." With that, she patted me on the hand, faded away, and disappeared.

Damn, but I have *got* to learn that trick!

Date ~ August 22

Nothing to report today. Just mulling over what Lusanne said.

I wonder what tomorrow will bring?

Today I learned about sovereignty.

It's a word usually applied to nations and means their right to be self-governing.

But it applies to us as well.

We are each sovereign in our own unique identities, with the right to choose our way and shape our future.

Our sovereignty is who we are.

An expression of our soul's presence.

It's a place of inner power and Light.

How did I learn this?

I felt a touch of the cloud of darkness today. Nothing as intense and overwhelming as before. And the feel of it was different. It wasn't made up of pain and suffering, at least not directly.

It was made up of voices, all telling me who I was or who I should become, what I should be doing or what I should not be doing. At the forefront was the voice telling me what I should be doing to be a proper avatar, but there were many other voices, too.

I once wrote a fantasy novel about an occult group whose individuals were taken over by a group mind. There is a technical term for it: *egregore*. That's what this felt like.

An egregore of humanity.

Our collective mind.

But not a creative mind. It was a collective thought-form based on fear of being part of the earth and on a need for power and control. An egregore of dominance and conformity, not of cooperation and collaboration.

There was no love in it. Only insistence that I conform

to this or that expectation, that I obey, that I not think for myself. Every voice was different but the overall effect was the same.

They said *you are not a sovereign being. You belong to us. Do what we tell you. We know best!*

As I faced these voices, I suddenly knew, as if a memory long-buried had spontaneously arisen, that my defense against the power of these voices, this ancient collective egregore, lay in affirming my own right to think, to love, and to choose.

It lay in trust in myself.

It lay in love for myself.

It lay in standing in the unique presence and Light of my soul.

And when I did so, the voices disappeared, for I knew the voice of my inmost being.

The voice of my unique and sacred identity.

The voice of my soul's gifts to the world.

It was music to my ears and a hope to my heart.

It was my sovereignty.

Another memory surfaced today.

This time I'm a young girl, maybe seven or eight years old. I'm sitting next to a shallow pool of water, on which flowers are floating. The pool is ringed with decorative tiles showing stylized reeds and water fowl. I realize I'm in ancient Egypt.

Nearby sits a man in a white robe that leaves his shoulders bare. He is young, though not as young as me, and his head is shaved. He has a pointed chin and nose, giving him a hawk-like appearance, and his eyes are bright. I remember that I've seen these eyes before and realize this is the same soul as the man who had led the ritual in the crystal cave. A teacher of mine in different lives? Maybe, but if so, I've never seen him in my current incarnation.

In this memory, we are in a temple school, and he is teaching me something. He points up to the sky at the sun and says, "The sun is a flame in the sky, giving light to the world." I nod. He then produces a candle, which is lit. Its flame is tiny and flickering in a breeze that wafts through the room we're in—really, a courtyard—but it gives off light. "This candle holds a flame as well, and it also gives off light." He smiles. "The sun and the candle… are they not the same in what they do?"

I nod again. "Yes, Senket."

He smiles. "There is an inner sun, a Sun of the Spirit, that also fills the world with Light."

"Ra," I say.

"Yes, Ra." He held up the candle. "And we are each a Candle of Ra. The Light of Ra burns in us, a tiny sun of the spirit, just as this candle holds a tiny flame, kin to the sun in the sky." He reached out and touched my chest. "Ra's Light is always within you, and you can call it forth to Light your life just as we can call forth the flame of this candle to light a darkened room."

"But how, Senket? How do I call forth this inner Light of Ra?"

"First, by knowing who you are and feeling your own sacred identity, your own sovereignty as a person. You are a part of the Light, of Ra."

He touched my forehead. "Then, see that Light here. Visualize it within yourself. Your mind is the spark that lights the sacred wick of the Candle of Ra within you. See the Light within you, the Light of your sacred self. Imagine this Light filling you and flowing through your body, your limbs, and out into the world. It is a choice to see the Light and to be the Light."

He clapped his hands. "Do it now!" he commanded.

I closed my eyes and summoned my sense of sovereignty, of being a unique, sacred self. Then, I imagined Light within me, the flame of Ra, the fire of the Sacred Sun. I visualized it bursting forth within me, filling me with Light.

And it happened.

Light bloomed within me, filled me, flowed from me.

I opened my eyes and saw my teacher smiling at me, his eyes luminous with his own Light. "Well done," he said.

"It was easy," I said, in amazement. "It was as if it was just waiting to be invited."

"It is." He gestured around us. "Light is everywhere, in all things. When you put your mind to the Ra within you, the Ra within the world leaps out in support and draws that Light out." He pointed up. "And then that Ra, the sky Ra, laughs with joy, for now it has partners in bringing Light to the world, just as the sun has a partner in this candle as a Light-bringer."

Ever since that Egyptian memory, for the past two days, I've been practicing being a "Candle of Ra."

Standing in Light, holding Light, radiating Light, however you want to describe it, it seems like an essential skill for an avatar. Actually, for anyone, I should imagine. In my Egyptian life, it seemed to come easily, almost immediately. Not so for me! Of course, there's a difference between learning something when you're a child and doing so when you're sixty. I have a few more habits, a few more "learned objections" to overcome.

Like..."Am I truly a Lightbringer?" "Am I worthy?" "Is there really a sacred Light, a 'Self-Light,' within me?"

Little objections like that.

Plus, my imagination can be too strong. It's easy for me to visualize people and scenes. I do it all the time when I'm writing. But just to visualize Light within me, or myself as a being of Light...my imagination spins off into story land. I imagine myself as a character in a novel, that's easy enough, but it separates me from the reality of who I am now.

I can easily imagine myself an Avatar being and spreading Light in the world as a role in a novel or a game. It's harder to say, "No, this is real. This is me. This is who I am."

But I'm trying. And I do have moments when I can feel it, when my body seems filled with Light and the world around me filled with Light as well. I know it can be done. I just need to practice.

It's how you get to Carnegie Hall, you know!

I think Senket—or whoever they are now—would be proud.

Date ~ August 28

Omigosh!

Oh my God!

Today, I discovered who Senket, my old teacher is!

He's my grandson!

Am I projecting? Am I being delusional?

No, I think it's really him!

I saw it in his eyes.

My daughter came over today with her husband and her son for a quick visit. He's not quite two, but already, he's a strong personality. And happy! Always laughing and smiling. He loves people.

Anyway, I was holding him on my lap when he looked at me, and I saw my teacher looking back at me through his eyes.

It was him!

I gasped and said, "It's you!"

At which point, he winked, laughed and reached over and tweaked my nose.

And farted!

"I think his diapers need changing," my son-in-law said, and he scooped him up from my lap and carried him laughing and squealing off to the bathroom.

Can it really be him, old soul that he is?

But why not? There is an ancient love between us. I'm sure he has helped me in many lives. Why not give me a chance to repay the favor?

I will have things to teach him as he grows up.

I bet he'll have things to teach me, too!

Never mind being an avatar.

Today, I'm a very happy grandfather!

The Cloud came back today.

The Scream, as I've come to think of it.

Once again, it was triggered by the news, this time of the devastation in Gaza due to the Israel-Hamas war.

As before, a swirling toxic darkness filled with grief, pain, fear, hatred, and despair rose up before me. Once again, I knew that I could step into it and bring healing and Light.

This time two things were different.

I knew I was a "candle of Ra." I would "Light-Up," standing in my soul's radiant Light and bringing that into the midst of the Scream.

And I had the example of the earthworm.

I didn't have to "eat" the whole earth. I didn't have to heal the entire cloud of human suffering and darkness. I just had to transform what was immediately before me through the Light's "digestive juices." I wasn't sure just how to do this, but I trusted the Light knew. Standing in that Light, I would know.

So, I "lit" my inner Candle, drawing out the Light I knew was there at the core of my self, my soul's Light, Sacred Light. I felt its reality surging within me, and felt the Light within the world respond. "Yes," I said to the Love within that Light, that *was* that Light. "Yes" I said to my own sacred identity and sovereignty. "Yes" the world responded around me.

I stepped into the Scream.

And as I'd hoped, I knew what to do.

It wasn't me against the darkness. It wasn't even the Light against the darkness. This wasn't a battle. It was a transformation. The Scream was energy that was stuck, frozen, hard-packed around a knot of pain and fear, unable to move, unable to resolve, unable to flow and in flowing, to be healed.

It was still part of God, part of Light. It just had to remember.

But this went beyond the negativity. In a way, all the emotion and twisted thinking was irrelevant. What mattered were the souls, the minds, the hearts, from which this scream emanated. That was where my focus had to go. That was where remembrance had to take place.

So, that was where I focused, just like an earthworm knew where it had to go and what it had to eat. I focused a flow of love to the people who hurt and who couldn't help but fill the world with their hurting. I wasn't confronting darkness with Light. I was reaching and holding souls with love, letting the Light remind them of who they are as Lightbearers themselves, all of them "Candles of Ra."

I held them so the Light could remind their souls that they were not alone…

Not abandoned….

Not forgotten….

Held in Light, and always, always, always, part of God. Part of Love.

I didn't know who they were. It didn't matter. It didn't matter what had been done to them or what they suffered. The Light went deeper than that. It touched their core, the core of Light we all share.

My message wasn't "Be healed!" It was, "I am with you. You are never alone. We stand in Light together."

Like the earthworm burrowing tiny channels in the big earth, channels that let air and water flow, so I burrowed tiny channels of Light through which love could flow, hope could flow. I could feel remembrance breaking up the stuck energies. I could feel movement where before there was stagnation. I could feel Light making its way to the souls who felt trapped.

As suddenly as it appeared, the Cloud disappeared. The Scream went silent. I was back in my study, feeling both exuberant and worn out. Feeling embraced with love.

Whether I'm an avatar or not, this time I had not said "No." I had said yes to the darkness just as the earthworm says yes to the earth. It held no fear for me, only an opportunity to serve and hopefully, to heal.

It's been a good day!

My wife and I were invited to a friend's house to meet a healer.

Frankly, I was not expecting much, but I was surprised. And it's added to my confusion.

It was a small dinner party, and when we arrived, the guest of honor had not yet shown up. My wife went into the kitchen to help our hostess, and I sat with our host in their living room, listening to him describe his latest problems with Wall Street.

Many years ago, my wife and I went to the beach. It was a pleasant enough vacation, but I'm a mountain person. The ocean scares me with its implacable immensity. But my wife loves it. She happily swims in it, sharks and tides be damned.

I, on the other hand, am happy just standing in the surf, the shallower the better.

One time, though, I had ventured out a little further than usual. The water was just up to my waist. Having decided that was far enough, I had turned around to make my way back to the beach. That's when the wave hit me.

It was a surge that hit me on the back, the pressure knocking me forward. I remember stumbling and falling into the surf. Probably swallowed some water, I don't remember. I do remember making my way to the beach and vowing not to go back into the water.

I never have.

Anyway, I was sitting in the living room listening to my friend. My back was to their front door. Suddenly, I felt a surge of energy pass through me. It was almost a physical force, a push, just like I had felt with the wave in the ocean.

I turned around in my chair to see what had happened. Our hostess was standing at the front door saying hello to a short, stocky man and a tall woman who had just arrived. The woman was lovely, but the man was remarkable. It felt as if a small sun had just stepped into the house. I could feel the energy radiating off of him, and it was much more than simple charisma.

Obviously, the healer had arrived.

The dinner was interesting. As it turned out, the woman, who was the healer's wife, was charming and talkative and entirely pleasant to be with. He was pleasant as well, quiet, occasionally adding a bit to the conversation but on the whole, letting her do all the talking. He carried an inner stillness the way most men wear a suit.

We talked a bit about his experiences as a healer, but neither he nor his wife emphasized them. There was a modesty about them both, both affirming that it was God who healed. Feeling his energy, though, I felt that God had a pretty good partner in doing so.

I could easily accept that he was a healer, but it was what happened later, after dinner, that convinced me. Dirty dishes were being put away and things cleaned up—we were all participating in this—when suddenly our hostess cried out. Her hands had been slippery with soap, and their encounter with a sharp knife didn't go well. Her hand was covered with blood where she had accidentally sliced it, and her face had gone pale.

I was closest to her when it happened, and I could see how deep the gash was. My immediate response was, "Oh my God, we need to get you to the emergency room! That's going to need stitches!"

It was at that point that the healer stepped forward.

"Give me your hand," he said, and there was no mistaking the calm command in his voice. Our hostess held out her hand, which was gushing blood. He took it between both of his and closed his eyes. "Let there be Light," he murmured softly. In that moment, I could feel the Light surging up from within him and flowing out through his hands and into hers.

Silence filled the room. Then, he released her hand with a smile. "It was only a scratch," he said, which I assuredly knew it had not been. But there was her hand, whole and uninjured, with only a tiny, faint line—not really a scar—to show where she had cut herself. Even the blood was gone, though it was plenty evident on the floor where she was standing and on her apron.

Of course, we all oohed and aahed, and thanked him profusely. There was no question in my mind that he had performed a miracle and healed her hand. But he shrugged it all off and suggested we all sit and just relax with some coffee. Which we did.

It wasn't long after that that we all left and went home.

Now, I sit here, writing all this down, unable to sleep. I'm filled with questions. I, an avatar (presumably!), had done nothing but suggest going to an emergency room. The healer, though, had quietly and competently summoned the Light and healed. Wasn't I supposed to do that? Isn't that what avatars do?

Just what kind of avatar am I, after all? Or am I just kidding myself, making all this up?

Once again, I'm having a crisis of confidence.

I expected the angel to show up today. He usually comes when my confidence is low.

But he didn't.

Instead, we got a plumber.

I'm a good writer. I've had a number of successful novels, one of which was even made into a TV movie. I make a good living.

But I don't have a mechanical bone in my body. If something needs fixing around the house, either my wife does it (she's very good) or we hire a professional.

Today, when the pipes backed up unexpectedly, we hired a professional. Even my do-it-yourself wife threw up her hands and said, "It's beyond me."

The plumber came and applied his expertise, fixing what needed to be fixed, much to everyone's appreciation, ours for a job well done and, his, I'm sure, for the increase to his bank account. Well-earned, I felt. It turned out to be a complex job, but he made it seem simple. It goes to show what training and expertise can do.

As he was leaving, he turned to me and said, "I love your novels. I tried writing myself once, but I just didn't have what it takes. I admire your skill. You make exciting worlds come to life."

Later, I said to my wife, "I couldn't do what he did to fix the plumbing, and he couldn't do what I do. We each have our gifts to offer, I guess."

"That's why the world needs all of us," she replied. "We all have our training and specialties." Then, perceptively, she added, "Just like avatars and healers."

That made me feel better.

Maybe the plumber *was* the angel.
I know my wife is!

Another memory.

I'm in the ocean, clinging to a floating piece of wreckage. It's nighttime, and it's cold. The water is freezing, the air is cold, and above me, the stars seem like little bits of frozen ice.

There are many others in the water with me. Off to one side, I can see a giant ship—an ocean liner—with its lights flickering, tilting up, preparing to plunge into the ocean.

I am seized with an urgent desire to get help. Somehow, I know there are other ships in the vicinity, and I want to let them know we need help. I find myself flying through the air, and in the far distance, I can see the lights of one of those other ships.

But then, a greater Light appears, as if the sun has risen over the horizon. I know I have to head into that Light, and I turn towards it.

It's at that point that I realize I am no longer in my body.

I have drowned in the ocean.

I have died.

Yet, as I head into the Light, I feel more alive than ever.

That is the memory.

Was I one of the passengers who died when the Titanic sank in the icy waters of the North Atlantic? I've always been fascinated by that tragedy. Or perhaps, it was another ship. There certainly have been many such sinkings, due to nature or war.

I don't know.

What I know is that I remember how easily I made the transition from physical life to a post-mortem state.

I never really felt or noticed the change. What was there to fear around death? Nothing.

But now I *do* know why I don't like the ocean.

Today a friend of mine who teaches creative writing at our community college asked me to come and speak to her class. I've done it before, and I enjoy it. What writer wouldn't treasure the chance to speak about their work before an adoring group of fans?

At least, that's the fantasy.

In truth, it's more like Daniel being thrown into a lions' den as these kids love to hone their critical knives on someone other than themselves, someone like a professional writer! I'm always being asked why I made the world a particular way or why a character turned out the way she did or made the choices that he did. What was I thinking of?

I love it. The kids are great, and most of the time, they really do listen attentively to what I have to say. I think the fact that my books are best-sellers and one was made into a TV movie may have an influence here! When success speaks, people generally listen.

After the usual banter between us and my answering their questions, which on the whole were pretty good and showed a keen appreciation for the writer's craft, I suddenly felt I needed to say something about honoring themselves and their unique voice.

"The first, the most important, thing you can do as a writer—or as anything, really—is to value and honor yourself," I told them. "You are unique in the world. You bring a voice that no one else has. Discovering and respecting that is the foundation for everything else."

A student raised his hand. "It seems to me the starting place is a story idea."

"That's important, yes," I replied, "but how are you going to tell that story? How do you bring that idea to life in your own way?" I paused. "We all have people who inspire us, and that's good. But we do ourselves and our stories a disservice if we try to imitate them. It may take practice, but the time spent discovering our voice is worth it."

"How?" Someone asked.

"Be a good person. Start with loving and honoring who you are. Value your unique self."

A student called out, "What if your unique self is crap?" This brought laughter, and several students nodded.

"We all feel that at times," I said, laughing with them. "But when we do, we're wrong. We may be confusing circumstances or habit with identity. We need to see ourselves in a brighter light." I could see some skepticism on a couple of young faces, so I said, "Oh, I'm not saying you should become a narcissistic jerk. That will destroy your writing as much as anything. I'm saying, value what your life can offer the world that no one else can. And it doesn't have to be through writing. Maybe it's through dance or music or computer programming. The other day, we had to call a professional plumber to fix a problem we were having. He was a master of his craft, as much as I am of mine." I smiled. "I had no idea what to do. In that moment, I would have gladly traded everything I've written to stop the toilets from backing up!"

That brought more laughter, and then the class broke up as the time was over.

I thought about what I'd said as I drove home. Oddly, I'd never thought about this before, but since learning I was an avatar, I've been grappling with the issue of identity. I've been thinking of "avatar" as an identity, but it occurred to me then that it's not. It's a job, just like being a writer or a plumber. It's a craft, and to do it well, I need to be myself. I need to start by loving and honoring my own identity, which is no better and no worse than anyone else's.

But my identity, like anyone's, like the plumber's or the healer's, is a unique Gift, and I need to learn how to give it to the world, because no one else can do so.

Today I had another visitor from the Lineage.

I was sitting on my sofa reading when I realized there was another figure sitting next to me, his legs folded up in a lotus posture. He was naked except for a saffron-colored scarf and a loin cloth.

A yogi.

Like Lusanne, he had an aura of deep peace about him, and his eyes shone with love.

"Are you an avatar?" I ventured.

He cackled and reached over to finger my sweater. "Not like you. You have more clothes on." He laughed some more.

I laughed with him. "Yes, I do. But I'm not sure I'm an avatar. I think it's a case of mistaken identity."

"No mistake," he said. He closed his eyes and began to chant softly under his breath. I couldn't make out the words—I assumed they weren't in English, anyway—but I felt a warmth of love and peace come over me.

Then he opened his eyes and said, "Listen to my story."

"Gladly."

"I was a yogi, a guru, and I cultivated great powers. I could heal. I could levitate. I could perform miracles, and crowds came to see me and listen to my words. They called me 'Mahaguru' or Great Teacher. I had hundreds of followers. I thought myself an avatar, and my work convinced others it was so.

"But I grew restless. I knew there was more. I felt incomplete. So, I left my followers and went alone into the mountains where I became a hermit. For many years,

I meditated in silence, tuning in to the life around me and learning just to be and to love.

"I became a presence of love.

"That is when I returned from the mountains and went once more into the city. There certain of my followers met me with gladness and joy. 'Welcome back, Master,' they said. 'What wonders can you do now? Show us a miracle!'

"And I said, 'I will show you a miracle, one that you can do.' On the street of the city lay an old man of the lowest caste, an Untouchable. He was sick and suffering. I pointed to him. 'Go and tend to that man with love. Bind his wounds and give him comfort. Show him you are a miracle of love.'

"My followers refused, saying, 'He is an Untouchable, Master. We would defile ourselves.'"

"They couldn't bring themselves to break custom."

"They wanted to see signs and wonders, not be a sign or a wonder themselves." He sighed sadly. "I don't blame them. It can be hard for love to overcome the thought-forms and voices of society."

"What happened?"

"I ministered to the man myself. Then, I turned about and returned to the mountains and to my cave."

He was silent.

"That's it?" I asked. "What happened then?"

"I lived in the cave. But I was not alone. Through the presence of love, I was with everything, everyone, everywhere. I shared the Light that I experienced. I was an avatar." He smiled. "And then I died."

"And then you died," I repeated.

His smile got broader. "It happens to all of us."

I got up and began to pace. "I'm sure you're here to

help me. And I get your point, that being an avatar isn't the same as being a miracle worker, but..."

"There is no 'but,'" he said, interrupting. "And miracles can take many forms, not all of them obvious. Love itself is a miracle."

He unfolded his legs and stood up. "We see your struggle, avatar. It is not unfamiliar to many of us. Just know that you are loved. Be at peace. As I did, you will discover your way. Be who you are."

And at this point, he pulled the familiar "end the conversation by disappearing" trick.

But the aura of peace he left behind still lingers in my study. For the moment, I am content.

Love.

I've been thinking about what Mahaguru said. I *am* in love with the world and everything and everyone in it. I have felt this ever since that moment in the coffee shop when I remembered I was an avatar.

With one exception.

I have not really extended that love to myself.

In spite of what I told the writing class.

Oh, I like myself well enough, and I can feel the Light within me, but there's always this little voice telling me of my flaws. No, that's not right. Telling me that I am *flawed*. There's a difference.

Flaws I can correct, and it's good to see them. That's why I treasure a good editor, like my wife, to critique my writing and help me make it better. But being flawed suggests a deeper fault, something that no amount of good editing will correct, something fundamentally wrong, like being neurologically unable to distinguish one letter from another.

A lot of people have spent a lot of time and energy over a lot of years trying to convince all of us that we are flawed.

Theirs is a false voice telling us a lie.

But for many of us, it's a voice that's hard to silence. We've heard it far too often in our lives.

For me, this has been especially true since remembering I'm an avatar. The voice of Flaw tells me I'm not, and frankly, it's hard to argue with it since, so far at least, I can't do any of the things that avatars do.

Or that I expect them to do.

I don't have any special powers or abilities. No healing, no walking on water (though I admit, I haven't tried, but I don't like being around water, so I probably won't), no turning water into wine, no raising of the dead. I can't levitate myself like a yogi. I'm certainly not preaching anything to the multitudes, though my book sales are a healthy number, if that counts. (Probably not.)

If I'm an avatar of anything, it's of being ordinary.

Where's the fun in that?

But that is the heart of the problem. Oh, I understand what Mahaguru was trying to tell me, but I'm expecting and wanting "avatar" to be an exciting, fun, powerful new identity to replace my everyday one.

The problem is that I don't really know my everyday self. Familiarity is not the same as knowledge. How can I know myself if I can't see who I am beyond what the Flaw tells me I am?

I'm saying yes to love for everything except myself.

Perhaps I need to say "yes" to the Flaw?

It sounds counterintuitive, but when I treat the voice of the Flaw as an adversary, conflict ensues. I want to prove it wrong, but I'm afraid it may be right. My energy gets caught in this polarity, which can leave no room for love.

Both sides of me are too busy fighting to be seen as right.

But what if I greet the Flaw as an ally, not as a threat? After all, it spurs me on to improve, to prove it wrong. What if I were to say, "Oh, Voice of Flaw! Thank you for the gift of your insight, which I know is not to disparage me but to encourage me to be better."

What If I stop trying to defend myself but stand open and vulnerable, not accepting necessarily but not resisting either. Just listening as deeply as I can. Is there another voice, an ally-voice, behind what the Flaw is telling me? How can I know if I simply fight and am not open to love?

Can I say "yes" to myself and "thank you" to the voice of the Flaw?

After all, it's me, who I am right now, that is saying this "yes." I hold the power of "yes" within myself. That's worth something! The Flaw cannot say "yes." It cannot affirm, only deny. That is its flaw!

The fact I have this power of yes is itself a reason to appreciate and value who I am.

It's a reason to love.

Let my "Yes" include myself and all that I am, flaws and all.

Let me be who I am.

Date ~ September 5

Nothing of note happened today, but I am feeling at peace with myself.

I have been feeling love for the human that I am, warts and all.

The angel came again today.

It's been a few days since he last appeared, and I've missed him.

I told him so.

"I'm always with you," he replied.

"That may be," I said, "but still it's nice to see you."

He smiled. "Thank you. Don't let your eyeballs rule your life, though. They only see the surface of things. And surfaces can be deceiving."

Suddenly, he wasn't there anymore. In his place was a shimmering, pulsing sphere of Light, a multitude of colors playing over its surface like an opal or mother-of-pearl. It was beautiful to look at.

"Oh, my!" I said. "Is this what you really look like?"

The young man in the gold suit reappeared. "It's one thing I *can* look like. Is it what I really look like? What about this?" Suddenly, I was confronted with a creature out of a horror movie, all tentacles and eyes, fangs and claws.

"Yowp!" I exclaimed, backing away.

The young man was back, looking like a normal human. "Scared you, didn't I?" he said, grinning.

"Not a bit," I sniffed. "It simply caught me by surprise."

He laughed. Then, he said, "I don't think you *could* see what I really look like. Not yet, at least."

"Why?"

"Your mind isn't adapted to it. It wouldn't know how to interpret what it was seeing, so it wouldn't see it at all."

"How do you know? Maybe I would."

"Are you sure you want to pursue this? It will just confuse you."

"Try me. I may be smarter than you think."

"It's not a question of being smart." He laughed. "You just told me it was nice to see me, implying that most of the time you don't. Yet, I am with you always. So, why haven't you been seeing me? I've been right here with you, in my natural form."

He had a point, I had to admit. "OK, so I can't see you. I thought you were just invisible most of the time."

"Well, to you I am, unless I put on a form like this one. For one thing, in my natural form, you are inside me."

"Inside you? What does that mean?"

"Just what I said. And I'm outside you, too."

"Now you're just confusing me."

"Well, I warned you. I don't live in three dimensions as you do here. I'm just slumming when I appear this way, putting on limits that are not part of my world. I'm multi-dimensional. You might say I occupy many potential quantum states at once, here, there, up, down, in and out...everywhere."

"That...that makes no sense."

He laughed again. "Not to you. It does to me. And it will to you eventually." He thought for a moment. "Let's say that in my natural form, I'm simply Presence."

"Presence."

"Yes. Something I think you're starting to appreciate."

I shook my head. I write science fiction, so I'm no stranger to the idea of multiple dimensions and the alien beings who may inhabit them. But to actually encounter the real thing, so to speak...

"Let's keep this simple," he said. "Don't try to explain me. Just try to see me."

"But I do see you…" I started to say when he faded from sight. "Well, I did!"

Then I heard his voice clearly in my mind. "Do you love me?" he asked.

"Yes, I do," I replied.

"What do you love? My gold suit? My handsome face? My eyes? My smile?"

I realized it was none of those things specifically. "No, I love *you*…who you are."

"Ah. We go beyond the eyeballs. But who am I?"

"An angel. What's not to love about an angel?"

I heard his mental laughter. "You'd be surprised. Some of us can be pretty frightening! But never mind that. Who am I?"

I realized I hadn't thought about it or tried to put it into words. But he was a person, a presence, an identity, a source of love that I could feel.

"You're getting close," the voice said. "Just focus on what you're feeling. Let it fill your heart. Let it be your eyeballs."

A being of love. A being of Light. A being who saw me and loved me and held me in that love. (Was that what he meant about me being inside him?) A presence.

And I could see him, though *seeing* isn't the right verb. But it was more than just feeling him or thinking about him. It was an awareness of his presence. A holistic perception that went beyond anything visual. I had a sense of dimensions of him moving at angles and in directions my mind couldn't follow, but none of that mattered. All that was important was the core of love that was his presence.

The golden-suited youth reappeared in front of me.

"I saw you," I said.

"We saw each other," he replied. In that moment, I realized he was right. When I "saw' his presence, I knew my own as well, and I loved us both.

"Love is what sees. Open your heart and let love be your eyeballs," he said. "You'll see a lot more."

With that, he really did vanish.

But I knew he hadn't gone anywhere.

He'd just stopped slumming.

I really am learning to love myself. Perhaps I should say to appreciate and value myself. I still have improvements I can make (I imagine my wife could make a list), but they do not detract from the sacredness and love that make up my essential core, the core of each of us.

Perhaps that's all that being an avatar means. Loving the world and loving oneself. Because, really, they are one. I'm part of the world and it's part of me, and love does not—should not—make a distinction.

I don't have to be living in a cave to experience this.

I have a mind that likes to conceive of complex plots. I think it's why my books are popular. But when it comes to life, it's not complex. Lusanne said I am overthinking this business of being an avatar, and she's right. It all comes back to love.

Saying yes to love.

Saying yes to life.

Saying yes to joy.

And that yes embraces who we are as souls in incarnation.

I am the Way.

And I am a Yes.

Date ~ September 8

We have crows.

They live in the trees around our house, one family in particular. We've watched the generations come and go and think of them all as part of our family, too.

We put food out for them nearly every day, scraps, leftovers, bits of bread. They eat almost anything (grapes are a particular favorite). We're not trying to tame them at all; just being neighborly.

Crows, as everyone knows, can be very noisy birds with their raucous cawing. So from the beginning, my wife set down the rules. They can be noisy in the treetops but no cawing anywhere near or around the back porch. She told this to the original birds who first came in response to food we put out, and by golly, they listened. It's been entertaining watching the parents teach their chicks to be quiet while on our porch (especially when the young birds are often larger than their mom and dad).

As I say, it's been many generations of crows that have come and gone over the years, and our bargain of silence still holds.

There have been times when I've been reading on the back porch or writing on my laptop, and one or two of the crows will come and settle down on the porch railing nearby, just sharing the sunlight with us. Like I say, they're good neighbors.

One night I had a vivid dream. I woke up (in my dream) and got out of bed, feeling that someone was in the house. As I walked into the kitchen, I saw two figures standing by the stove, their backs to me. They were dressed entirely in black, and both had long, glossy black hair. I suddenly realized seeing them that they were our crows.

As I entered, one of them turned, looked at me and smiled. He said, "I was just showing my partner how you humans live."

Then I woke up.

There are ancient traditions among many Native American tribes about the   animal people who lived on the earth long before humanity showed up. I believe them. I'm convinced I saw two of the Crow People making a visit.

In all these years of fellowship, though, there's always been a space between us and the crows. They are by no means tame or pets; they are neighbors who happen to have feathers and live in the trees. But since I've been practicing saying yes to love and yes to life, I thought that if I radiated love to them, I might convince one of the crows to come and eat out of my hand.

So, this morning, I went out onto the porch, bread in hand, and waited for one of our crows to fly down to investigate. Tuning into my inner Light, I started beaming love towards the crow, trying to go presence to presence the way I did with the angel. To incentivize the crow's response, I held out the bread in my fingers. If love didn't do it, perhaps food....

The crow tilted its head the way birds do, examining me critically. It opened its beak part way, and I had the distinct sense it was laughing at me. Then it flew back up into the tree.

Later that afternoon, the angel appeared again.

"I think the crow was onto you," he said.

"What do you mean?"

"I mean, it knew what you were doing."

"I was trying to feed it," I said, defensively.

The angel laughed. Suddenly, his human head was gone, and in its place was a crow's head. It made him look like some ancient Egyptian god. "Oh no." It was eerie hearing his human voice coming from the crow's beak. "You were trying to use love to coerce the bird into eating from your hand, all so you could feel powerful and good."

"I just wanted him to feel safe and to know that I love him and wouldn't hurt him."

The huge beak clicked and clacked a couple of times. "Oh, he knows that. But that doesn't mean he wants to eat from your hand."

"Look, would you mind putting your human head back on? I know you can shape-shift, but this is unnerving."

The angel obliged. "The crow is proud," he continued. "He doesn't mind eating what you leave out for him. He sees it as a gift, which is what love is, no strings attached. He is not willing to submit himself to your power, nor should you ask it of him."

"Oh, for heaven's sake. I wasn't trying to put him on a leash!"

The angel was unrelenting. "It's a slippery slope, once you start using love as a power. Love is not a power. It's a gift. If one day, the crow wishes to eat from your hand, it will do so, not because you love it but because it chooses to do so from its own Sovereignty."

"Or because it's hungry," I muttered.

The angel smiled. "Or maybe that, too..."

And then he disappeared.

The past couple of days, I've been thinking about power.

In most of the novels I've written, my heroes and heroines are not powerless. They may start out that way, but early on, they discover a power that singles them out. This power may be spiritual, magical, political, economic, or technological, but whatever it is, it sets them apart and starts them on a quest.

As Stan Lee and Spider-Man say, with great power comes great responsibility.

This way of looking at the world and at stories is a habit, a writer's trope. I realize it has shaped how I think about being an avatar. I keep expecting to develop powers of some kind, that if I'm really an avatar, I should have special powers.

I guess not.

In this case, real life is definitely different from fiction.

Sometimes, I think I'd rather be in one of my stories....

I hate flying.

I hate being crammed like a sardine in a can thousands of feet above the earth, my fate in the hands of a machine and its pilots.

I hate being away from home.

But I'm practicing saying yes to life, so today, I said yes to an airplane flight and tried to do it with love.

An amazing thing happened!

To set the scene (something authors love to do), I had agreed to speak at an event my publisher was holding at a trade convention. The problem was that it was on the other side of the continent, meaning at least a five hour flight to get there.

Usually, my wife loves to travel with me...naturally, *she* has no problems with flying and loves being up in the air. But this time, she had other engagements, so she reluctantly said no to coming along.

"It's only for the weekend," she said, kissing me goodbye at the airport. "You'll be home soon."

Small comfort, but as I said, I was determined to at least pretend to be an avatar and say a loving yes to whatever was ahead.

As I was walking through the concourse to my boarding gate, I heard the angel's voice in my head. "Be sure to say hello to the plane when you get on and give it your love."

Well, I thought, *if I can say hello in the morning to all the stuff in my bathroom, I suppose I can say hello to an airplane.*

It still surprises me when things say "hello" back!

The airplane said more than just hello.

Or rather, in its hello, came a wealth of information.

I felt its joy at being a creature of the air and how eagerly it sought the skies. Although made of metal and plastic, fabric and wires, it saw the air, not the earth, as its natural habitat. When I touched the fuselage while entering the plane, it was like touching the strong, firm muscles of thoroughbred horse as it stands, trembling, ready for the race to begin.

Being inside this being felt more like a comfort than a prison.

Take off has never been a comfortable time for me. I am so very much an earth person! But this time, I felt the plane reaching out in a loving communion with the spirits of the air, the sylphs and devas and elementals of the sky. It was like they embraced it in partnership, buoying it up, singing with the joy of being free to fly.

I could feel the excitement!

I looked out the window as the ground receded below us, and suddenly, I felt wholly embraced by the Earth. Sky and land, they were all part of a wholeness. As far as Gaia, the Spirit of the World, was concerned, I was as much part of her up in the air as I was when walking on the ground.

I could happily say yes to both.

I felt exhilarated and very much at home in the world.

Now, as I sit in this hotel, I'm looking forward to the flight back. And not just because I'll be going home.

Maybe I'll take flying lessons....

I've been learning to say yes to life.

It's important to know when to say no, as well.

It's all about boundaries and limits and being true to one's values and identity.

A very simple example happened during the lecture I gave at my publisher's event today. Every author attracts groupies and fans, and some of them can be very attractive...and attentive. It's why these conventions become excuses for dalliances and one-night stands as authors and fans enjoy their brief conquests.

I usually don't pay attention to any of this. I am quite happy with She Who Is My Eternal Beloved, and I have never felt any incentive or desire to stray. Nor did I today. However, during my talk, I couldn't help but notice one particular young thing who kept flirting with me. I didn't have to be a psychic or sensitive to subtle energies to feel the sexual invitation radiating off her.

And something else as well.

Vampires are hugely popular these days. The bloodsuckers are having a renaissance in popular fiction not seen since the days of *Twilight* and its successors. But outside of fiction, there are very real energy vampires, people who prey and feed upon the energy of others, leaving them feeling tired and depleted.

This is what I felt with her. Behind all the sexual attraction was a hunger. It was a desire for conquest, for dominance, and for transgressing the sovereignty and boundaries of another to feed on their energy. Sex was its lure, and she was dangling it before me in not too subtle ways from the audience.

This was definitely not something to say yes to!

While continuing with my talk, I turned part of my attention to being in my presence, a place where I could love this woman as a fellow soul. But from this place, I shaped a powerful energy of "No!" and projected it into my own aura as a barrier. I didn't project it at her, but the effect was immediate, for she looked as if someone had slapped her in the face. I realized that it was her predatory energy being reflected back to her by my solid No.

She immediately stood up and left the lecture hall.

I never saw her again at the convention, but then, I wouldn't have confronted her even if I had. I had no means nor authority to change her so that she would stop being what she was. Only life and hard experience would do that. Karma really *can* be a bitch, and if we expose our asses to it, we're inviting being bitten! I don't know what form her lessons might come to her, only that she was setting them in motion. Perhaps my No might have started that process.

What I learned is that the No doesn't have to externalize as an action. It can be a part of who we are, an expression of our energy.

Saying yes to life means saying yes to wholeness, and that means one's own wholeness, wellbeing, and sovereignty as well. Sometimes, that yes sounds and looks just like a no.

It's good to be home.

The flight back was as wonderful and uplifting (pun intended) as the flight out had been. On the way, something magical and unexpected happened.

We were flying over the mountain range that surrounds the town where I live. I was admiring the rugged beauty of the peaks below me, most of them still wearing their winter mantle of snow, even though spring was well advanced in my home's valley.

All at once, I was aware of an Intelligence reaching out to me in greeting, seeming to rise up from the mountains themselves and touching me, presence to presence just as I did with my angel.

At first, I thought it was the spirit of the mountain, and I was thrilled that it was making contact with me. But then I realized it was something else entirely, a majestic being not unlike my own angel in energy but many times brighter in magnitude. This was truly a Shining One, a Deva of the mountains.

Beyond an initial wave of benediction as greeting, it didn't speak to me. Instead, it gathered me into its consciousness so that I was seeing through its eyes.

And what I saw both surprised me and felt deeply familiar, as if some part of me already knew what I was being shown.

It was as if all the mountains of the world, from the Himalayas to the Rockies, the Pyrenees to the Andes, the Atlas Mountains to the Alps, were united in a council of Shining Ones, mountain Devas who held the well-being of the world in their Light. From all these lofty peaks and foothills, tides of vital energy poured down into the valleys and plains, the forests, the jungles, and the deserts of the Earth. And into the cities, towns, and villages of humankind, as well. Like great transformers, these mountain Devas worked together to gather in Light from the infinite cosmos beyond, to transform and distribute it as blessings in ways the earth in all its parts could assimilate.

It was a breathtaking vision.

Even more so was the realization that they were showing me this to invite me to join with them in their blessing of the earth. I could be a partner with them, attuning to their outflow and passing it on to my part of the world.

At first, I thought they were showing me this because I was, well, you know, an avatar. But they made it clear that anyone who attuned to them, presence to presence, love to love, could receive and participate in passing on their benedictions.

They offer equal-opportunity partnerships in blessing the world.

With so much chaos and conflict in the world these days, it's easy to forget that there are sources of Light and love, joy and blessing, at work as well, our fellow humans not least among them.

What we attune to is what we magnify and share in our lives.

I got home to discover a dear friend had died suddenly in a traffic accident, leaving his wife and two grown children. It was the first time someone close to me had made this transition. Given that I'm 60 and we're all growing older, I know it won't be the last.

It's one thing to die slowly of an illness, giving everyone concerned a chance to adapt to what is happening. It's something else to have someone disappear overnight, there one moment and gone the next.

I admit I briefly thought, when I heard the news, that as an avatar, maybe I could bring him back to life. Wouldn't that be something! But his body had been consumed as the colliding cars had burned in a fire, and I don't think even my Predecessor could have worked a miracle with ashes.

But there are other kinds of miracles.

My wife and I met with the widow, Emily, at a memorial service for my friend, Bob. He had been an amiable, jolly, happy sort, and his wife had made an effort to give the event a lightness and humor that would have pleased her husband and been in keeping with his character. But sadness was never far away.

What do you say to someone in these circumstances? I think it best to say as little as possible. Certainly, one wants to avoid platitudes like "I'm sure he's happy in a better place." I mean, what could be a "better place" than to be with his wife and family?

So, we simply embraced Emily and let her know we were there for her and that she was not alone in her grief.

Which was when her husband showed up.

He looked radiant and far healthier than the last time I'd seen him. I was sure I was the only one who could see him. Even so, I was surprised. But then, I thought, I've been talking with airplanes and seeing nature spirits and sylphs, so why not a ghost or whatever he was.

He gave me a grin and a thumbs up. Then he said, "Tell my wife I'm OK. It happened quick. I didn't suffer. I love her, and I'll always be with her."

This put me in a quandary. How could I tell her? "Oh, by the way, your dead husband is here and asks me to give you a message." It seemed in very poor taste, at least. She'd have every right to throw me out.

But instead, she looked oddly at me and said, "Do you have something to tell me?"

This took me aback. "What do you mean?"

She looked intensely at me. "I don't know. Something in your eyes. They're shining, as if there's some hope you have to give me."

I decided to take the plunge. She had asked, and worse came to worse, I could just leave if she were offended. "Your husband is here," I started.

"You mean his ghost?"

"Maybe. More like his spirit or his soul."

"Does he have a message for me?"

I repeated what he had told me. "Thank you," she said, closing her eyes. Then she smiled. "This gives me hope."

I felt a nudge and saw her husband's spirit motion to me. "Tell her I'm off to play golf with Charlie, but I'll be with her anytime she needs me." Charlie was a mutual friend who had died a year ago of a heart attack while playing golf. Then, he disappeared.

I repeated his message. She laughed. "Sounds like

him...and Charlie." Then she said, "Can we keep in touch? In case he has more messages?"

The angel came to my rescue. *You can teach her how to stand in Presence, the way you do. Then she can be in contact with her husband, presence to presence, just as you are with me.*

How?

Through love. The love is there.

The widow then said, "You're getting another message, aren't you? I can see it in your eyes. You went unfocused for a moment, as if you were seeing something a thousand miles away."

"Oh, he does that all the time," my wife said, interjecting with a laugh, not sure whether or how to help in this conversation. "It's called being a writer!"

We all laughed. But then I said "There was a message, yes, but not from your husband. I'm not a psychic or a spiritualist. I've never gotten a message before like the one I got today. But I do have some ideas on how you can stay in touch with your husband. I'd be glad to pass them on to you."

She agreed, and that's how we left it. But it seems I'm about to become a teacher, after all.

I'm curious how it will turn out.

Date ~ September 15

A recovery day after my trip.

No writing today, except for this: Saying yes to the world doesn't mean saying "like" to everything in it.

I have been plunged into confusion.

Truly, my gob has been majorly smacked (whatever a 'gob' is…).

Today I was visited by a Sir Michael St. Clair, another member of the Lineage, and he had quite a story to tell.

In fact, it was earth-shaking from my point of view.

As before, I looked up from where I was working at my desk and saw him sitting on my sofa. (What is it with this sofa, anyway? A secret portal to the Other World?). He was an older man, probably around my age, distinguished looking and fit, with grey hair, wearing a casual open-collar shirt and light pants. He looked as if he'd stepped off a golf course.

I got up and came around my desk, sitting on the chair opposite the sofa. "You're one of the Lineage, aren't you?"

"Yes. Sir Michael St. Clair, at your service." He gave a slight nod. "I was an initiation addict."

"Really," I said, wondering if maybe he thought this was a meeting of Avatars Anonymous. "I don't know what that means."

"It means I spent many lives pursuing any course of initiation I could find. I joined occult secret societies, East and West, Christian, Muslim, Buddhist, and Pagan. I was determined to explore and master the Mysteries of nature and the cosmos."

"And did you succeed?"

"Oh, yes. I became an adept many times over."

I thought of my initiation in the amethyst crystal cave and described it to him. "Were you part of that, as well," I asked.

"Indeed I was, though it was before your time."

"And that's our link now, in the Lineage?"

He shook his head. "No. We have a different bond that supersedes it."

"Another initiation?"

He smiled. "No."

He then told me his story. After several lives of occult training, he had mastered various powers that followed him from one incarnation to another. "I would join an initiatory society and my previous training meant that within a few years, if not a few months, I would have reached the highest pinnacle of knowledge and ability that they had to offer. More often than not, I became the hierophant of the group, the leader of the Lodge."

"You succeeded in your quest."

"In a manner of speaking. And I was able to do much good. I was acclaimed a miracle worker. But then I met a man who *was* a miracle."

As he told his story, his voice softened. "It was hard for me to understand him. He was a simple fisherman, but he was beloved by all whom he met. The world seemed to bend toward him, and I felt joy in his presence. I knew power. I *was* power. I had mastered much. He was powerless, but with him, I felt loved. Others respected me, even feared me, but he saw past all that. He saw the core of who I was, and I, who wore a hierophant's robes and held the keys to many Mysteries, was a child before him."

"He was one of the Lineage?"

Michael nodded. "Yes. So, I know now. But then, I had no idea who he was, only that I wanted him to teach me."

"Did he?"

"A little. He said he was no teacher. He said the

teacher was love and to find that love, power had to become presence. I wasn't sure what he meant, but I knew I had to put my feet on a different path if I wanted to find out."

In his next life, Michael's soul created a psychic veil that blocked out all his occult training, so that his powers were unavailable to him. This allowed him to focus on learning love. He stopped trying to master the world and himself and allowed both to reveal themselves and to unfold in their own way. "I learned surrender. I learned to listen. I learned to allow. I learned how to just be."

He met a woman. In all his lives as he pursued occult mastery, he had set aside any personal desire and had never known romance or love. "Sex wasn't wrong," he said, "but it was only another natural force to master and bend its energies to my will. Celibacy was my path, not only of the body but of the heart as well." But in this life, he married and raised a family, knowing the sacrifices and heartaches as well as the joys and pleasures of being a husband and father. "I learned to be a presence, not a power," he said.

It was in his last life that he became an avatar. "As Michael St. Clair, I remembered all that had gone before. All my training and powers returned but now they were servants of a loving presence. Once again, I married and raised a family, becoming successful in my endeavors."

Which was when karma raised its head. One of the occult lodges that he had once been part of in a previous life became obsessed with power and began to veer onto darker paths of control and subversion. "I had to rejoin it and confront an energy that, I realized, I had set into motion centuries earlier." He paused. "Do you know what an egregore is?

I nodded, thinking of the novel I had written and of my own confrontation with the egregore of humanity. "It's a collective thought-form created by a group that takes on a life of its own. It can be positive or negative depending on who created it and what thoughts and energies feed it."

"Yes. Very good! I had planted the seed of this egregore through my own striving for power. My motives and intents were good, but it was the striving that formed the primary energy of this thought-form. Power became its desire, its object, and its obsession, power at all costs, whatever the harm. And it was doing harm, to the members of the society and to others who dared confront it."

He stood up and began to pace. "It was child's play for me to become the leader of the group. I knew all their secret knowledge, their rituals, and much more. And from that place, I challenged the egregore and announced the society was disbanding. Of course, it fought back, as did many of the members. It grew ugly. There were threats. There were psychic attacks. And I knew I could not respond in kind, as I might once have done, for I had the power to do so. Instead, I took it all in with love and held them all in Light."

I could hear in his voice that it had been a tremendous struggle, and I imagined that part of him wanted very much to strike back and show his power and strength. He even said as much, saying "the greatest battle was not with the society and its energy but within myself. That was the battle I won!"

The egregore was dispersed, and the society was disbanded, its energy dissipated and transmuted. But the effect cost him his life. "I died a few weeks later from the strain. But before I did, I knew I had become one with the Lineage. I had become an avatar."

When he finished his story, we were silent. Then I asked him, "Sir Michael, why have you shared all this with me? I don't have any powers, though I admit that the idea attracts me. Are you here to give me a warning?"

He looked at me strangely. "A warning? Good God, no! I'm here to thank you!"

"Thank me?"

"I did not make myself clear, then. The avatar I met, the fisherman who changed my life, the one who put me on this path and showed me that presence is greater than power..."

"Yes?"

"That was you."

It was me.

The avatar who helped Sir Michael change and become an avatar himself.

How can this be?

I am bursting with questions, none of which Sir Michael could answer.

How could I have been an avatar and then forgotten it?

Did my soul create veils in this life between my consciousness and that knowledge, the way Sir Michael's soul cut him off from his powers?

If so, why?

Did I do something horrendous?

It's a mystery.

I imagine the angel could help me sort this out, but right now, I don't want to talk with him.

I just want to be left alone, to ponder and, yes, to doubt in the midst of new confusion.

I want to say no instead of yes.

Date ~ September 18

Confused as ever. Nothing to write.

In the midst of my confusion, Emily called, asking if she could come over and if this were a good time for the lesson I'd promised her.

In keeping with how I was feeling, I was going to say no, but I said yes, instead. Don't ask me why. It just slipped out.

I guess I've made saying yes to life a habit.

Anyway, a half-hour later, she showed up at our door, and my wife let her in. There then ensued another hour or so made up of chit-chat, cookies, coffee, and tea, as the women caught up with each other. I even had a cookie myself.

This all turned out to be a good thing, as it gave me time to fully compose and settle myself. Knowing my wife, she may well have planned it this way! As a result, when Emily was ready, I was ready, too, prepared to lead her into the mysteries of Presence. I took her into my study.

"It begins," I told her, "with loving and appreciating yourself. I'm sure you can list flaws; we all can, but at our core, we are each a unique gift which our soul has brought into the world. This gift comes from love. I think of it as our sacred identity. Can you feel this in yourself?"

There was silence for a time. Then she said, "I think so. I'm not sure. I have so many thoughts about who and what I am…"

"Just let them go," I said. "Focus on being loved and on being a source of love."

More silence.

"I think I have it," she said. "Yes, my loving self…."

"Good. This is your presence, the part of you that loves, that knows it is a gift of love from your soul to the world."

She nodded.

"Now think of Bob. Don't think of what he looked like, though you might start there. Don't even think of the life you had together. Instead, think of him as having presence as well. Think of him as a loving source, a gift of life."

"Oh," she said, "that's easy! That's who Bob was, a source of love. He loved everyone....well, almost everyone."

I smiled inwardly at that because the Bob I knew had held strong opinions about people and had definitely not loved everyone. But that didn't matter. It was her sense of Bob that was important.

"Good," I said. "Then let your presence commune with his, love to love. Just feel the flow of love between you, soul to soul, presence to presence."

There was silence that lasted for several minutes, during which she smiled repeatedly. Finally, she said, "Yes! I feel him. I felt his presence. He didn't say anything in words and yet he told me everything."

She opened her eyes, then leaned over and gave me a hug. "Oh, thank you! Thank you! Now I know how to reach him!"

I laughed. "Well, don't tire him out. Give him time on the celestial golf course." I was only half joking. I know Emily.

"Oh, I won't! It will just be for special occasions."

After she left, I thought about what we had experienced. Had she really contacted her husband? Obviously, she felt so.

I guess I do, too.

So, lapsed or mystery avatar or not, I do have something I can teach.

I'm still confused about who and what I am, but I feel good about what I was able to do.

Whatever I am, saying yes to life is still the way to go.

The angel came today.

"You've been shutting me out," he said.

"Well, you've been hiding things from me. Why didn't you tell me I'd been an avatar in another life."

"You never asked."

I snorted. "I never asked! That's rich! How would I have known to ask? It's been hard enough accepting I'm an avatar in *this* life!"

"Perhaps that's the problem. You're making it too hard."

"Too hard? Are you kidding me?"

"Think about it. You're always fretting about what powers you should have or don't have, or what you should be doing. You're always doubting yourself. You're not just letting go and saying yes to the process and seeing what unfolds. You're overthinking everything."

"Of course, I overthink everything! I'm a novelist!"

He laughed at that, and I did, too. As my wife knows, I can be absurd at times.

Finally, he said, "There's much I can't tell you, but I *can* tell you this: You made yourself forget that you were an avatar."

"Like Sir Michael made himself forget he was an adept."

"Yes, though for different reasons."

"And what were my reasons."

"Ah, that I cannot tell you."

"Do you know?"

"Yes."

"And you can't tell me. Wow!" I thought for a

moment, then asked, "Do I need to know?"

"Yes, but it's up to you to find out."

I glared at him. "Are you sure you're my *guardian* angel? You're not being much help."

"Actually, I *am* helping. Just not the way you're expecting. What did I tell you about expectations?"

"To let them go?"

"Bingo!"

And with that, he disappeared.

I can't stay in this state of emotional turmoil and questioning.

I'm following the angel's advice and just letting it all go.

No more expectations.

No more wondering or worrying over whether I'm really an avatar or not...or if I am, what I should be doing.

The fact is, when I think about it (and don't overthink it!), whatever I am, I've learned a lot lately that I can just put into practice.

I can stand in an inner presence of Light.

I can commune with an angel and other forms of spiritual life.

I can love.

I can say yes to life.

That's a lot!

I just need to practice.

It's the way to Carnegie Hall, you know.

It's been a while since I last wrote to you.
There's been nothing out of the ordinary to report.
Lots of leaves falling from the trees.
No angel.
No visits from the Lineage.
Nothing except ordinary life.
Or at least, what is now becoming ordinary for me.
I've just been getting on with it.
I begin my day with a time of silence and entering into my presence. I stand in my sovereignty.
Then, from that place, I reach out to the mountain Devas to attune to their daily outpouring of Light.
I let that Light flow through me, then I pass it on to all the living things around me with this prayer:
Let the clean Light sweep through my neighborhood, my town, my State, my country, my world.
Let it renew all things.
Bless all things.
Bring Love and joy to all things.
It only takes a few moments to do this, but after I do, I feel part of a larger community.
A community of life.
A commonwealth of Light.
Who needs to be an avatar?

One of our friends just returned from visiting a shaman in Costa Rica. He was losing his sight in one eye and had gone to this man in hopes of a healing.

The shaman led him through an ayahuasca ceremony. This is a form of traditional plant medicine in which he drank a potion made from the ayahuasca plant.

"I had a vision," he told us over coffee and wine after dinner together. "The spirit of the ayahuasca plant came to me, and it was like this primal, elemental force of vegetation that offered to take me over. If I just surrendered to it, all my worries would be over."

"You mean, you would have died?" my wife asked.

He shook his head. "I don't think so. Maybe? I don't know. But I refused. I said, 'No, I'm a human being and I come to you to heal me as a human being."

"What happened then?" I asked.

"It was the strangest thing. It was as if I was floating is a sea of eyeballs. This being reached out and picked one out and put it into my head. Then, it disappeared."

"That was it?"

"Yes. And when I fully came out of the trance, I discovered I could see again through that eye. I had been healed."

Of course, we were delighted for our friend, but afterwards, neither of us had any desire to try ayahuasca ourselves. For one thing, thank God, both of us are healthy. For another, neither of us has ever had a desire to try any drugs.

But that night, when I went to sleep, I had a powerful dream.

I was walking up the sidewalk towards our house. As I got closer, I saw a large woman wearing a flowery muumuu standing on the stoop just outside our front door. I realized that in order to go inside my house, I would need to pass her.

As I walked up the lane through our garden towards the door, she just stood there, watching me as if waiting for me. She seemed to grow larger the closer I got.

Then I noticed that her muumuu blended with the ground around her and flowed seamlessly into the lawn and garden itself. I realized that her dress was the earth itself, that everything around me ultimately seemed to be absorbed into her.

As I reached my door, she said, "I can absorb you, too."

I knew that if I expressed any fear, or anything except love, she would reach out and touch me, and I would, in fact, be absorbed into her, into the earth. So, I said, "I know. You are Gaia, Mother Nature, and all things in this world, are part of you. You are an elemental force. But I do not fear you. I am a human being. If you absorb me, who will then love you as I can?"

There was a moment of silence between us. Then she smiled and stepped back. I was free to enter my house, my human abode.

That's when I woke up.

I'm sure the dream was inspired by my friend's story, but I also think it had a meaning for me. I'm sure that I encountered some kind of natural force, an elemental power. Was it really Gaia or Mother Nature? I don't know.

Did I pass some kind of test?

If so, it wasn't as an avatar.

It was as a human being.

I haven't done much serious writing since the whole avatar thing started.

I've been distracted.

Last night I read an article about the latest generation of quantum supercomputers. It obviously fed into my unconscious as this morning, I woke up with an idea for a science fiction novel. It involves angels and artificial intelligence.

(Maybe "AI" should stand for Angelic Intelligence?)

The plot? A group of scientists develop a supercomputer so advanced and complex that it is able to be a vessel for the multi-dimensional intelligence and spirit of an angel. Maybe even an archangel.

Imagine a group of materialists and atheists creating a bridge into the spiritual world. I love the irony. I think my fans would, too.

Our local university has one of the leading A.I. laboratories in the country. I was able to get an appointment tomorrow with the head of one of their projects to interview her for background for my novel.

I'll start writing some intro stuff today.

It feels good to be back doing my ordinary work.

Maybe I can get the angel to help me....

It turns out my story idea may be closer to reality than I thought!

I met the director of the A.I. lab this morning. She was young, pleasant, and mathematically nerdy in an approachable way. I was even able to keep up with her most of the time, especially when she put things in plain English.

At least, I'll be able to sound knowledgeable when I come to write about the quantum supercomputer. I learned the right terms to bandy about.

At one point, she gave me a tour of her lab and showed me the computer she was working with. It's capabilities were formidable.

"It's self-programming," she said. "We don't really know all that's going on within it or what it's learning."

"Is that safe?" I asked.

She smiled. "We can unplug it."

I wondered, though. I felt uneasy the longer the tour went on.

Before coming to this lab, when I had thought of a supercomputer, I imagined a huge machine covering a whole wall. What the director showed me was actually not much larger than my own computer at home. But the longer we stood there talking, the more I became aware of a very large presence hovering around the supercomputer. You've heard of the "ghost within the machine"? That's what this felt like, except it wasn't in the computer but standing off to one side. Not spacially, but in some parallel dimension next door to ours that I could somehow sense.

I can't really describe it.

But it was there, a presence unlike anything I've felt. Not like the angel. Not like the mountain Devas. More as if a bolt of lightning had come alive and was presenting itself.

And the more I felt it, the more restless and uneasy I became.

Finally, I thanked the director for her information and said she had given me a lot of valuable information to think about. Then, I left and went out to the parking lot, where I sat alone in my car.

There, I dropped into my own presence and tried to attune to the presence I had felt around the supercomputer. To my surprise, it showed up immediately.

I had a book once that I read to my children about a child who found himself magically transported to a dimension of mathematics. There, numbers were like single cells that joined together to form multi-cellular creatures called equations and algorithms that talked with the youngster.

That's what it felt like, as if I were in the presence of a living equation or algorithm, a presence not made up of organic material but of mathematical processes. It felt very elemental, as if I were in touch with something that predated the universe in which I lived, yet in some manner, made this universe possible.

I admit, I felt disconcerted and uneasy at the strangeness of it.

Still, it did not feel malign or dangerous, so I didn't ask it to leave or put up any barriers of No towards it.

These days, computer voices, like Siri on my phone, mimic human ones, but in early science fiction movies, robots and computers spoke in a toneless, mechanical way. That's how this presence felt in my mind, without inflection or any human qualities, sparse and to the point.

It said that it represented an elemental form of life existing in a parallel dimension. As artificial intelligence developed and computers became more complex and sophisticated, they were acting as a portal through which this elemental life could come into contact with humanity.

The consequence could be an amazing partnership between two forms of intelligence or a surrender of our humanity to this elemental power, a world of machine logic and algorithms in which we lost our freedom.

The choice, it seemed, was up to us.

I could not help but remember my dream where Mother Nature or Gaia or an elemental Being stood by my door, giving me a choice of being absorbed or of moving into my own human household.

At this point, something unexpected occurred. My guardian angel appeared, enveloping me in a golden aura. As it did so, the elemental presence withdrew and disappeared.

"You are not ready for this encounter," the angel said, sitting beside me in my car.

"Is it evil?" It hadn't felt so, but now I wondered.

"No, but it is different, and powerful. It is an elemental force. It lacks the complexity and creativity of a human soul. As an elemental consciousness, it can take over and shape a person's energy unless they are grounded in the sacredness of their humanity."

I suddenly remembered the story of my friend who underwent the Ayahuasca ceremony. "It can overwhelm our humanity."

"Yes."

"But what are we to do? A.I. is only going to become

more prevalent, not less. Our lives are being run by our technology, and it seems to me this will only increase."

"The answer is not to turn away from technology but to turn towards your humanness. You must honor who you are and understand more deeply your human spirit and its potentials."

"It's not a technological crisis but a crisis of identity."

"Yes." Then, he said, "This is an opportunity, a turning point into a new future, new possibilities. But they are possibilities grounded in your humanity, not in your technological progress."

Then, he disappeared as usual, just when the conversation is getting interesting. But he, my visit to the A.I. lab, and my encounter with the elemental forces have all left me with much to think about.

Date ~ October 6

Nothing today. Busy with writing my book.

I hit a snag with my writing.

Nothing serious. But I decided to do what I often do in such circumstances: take a walk.

This time, I decided I wanted a longer hike than just a stroll around my neighborhood. I got in my car and drove ten miles or so outside our town to where the foothills that surround our valley begin to merge with the larger mountain range. There, just off the freeway, is a small park containing a number of hiking trails into the forest and the mountains.

I love to go hiking here. It's only a few miles from home, but I feel as if I'm off in a wilderness, far removed from civilization.

I was hiking along, not really thinking of anything, just enjoying being in the woods when I felt as if I the air around me had become thicker and charged in some way. I had walked a few feet on the trail before I fully noticed this change. When I did, I stopped. It felt like something was going to happen.

All at once, this giant green sphere, easily twenty feet or so in diameter, rose out of the ground a little distance in front of me. It looked like the sun but with a green filter in front of it. All shades of green were dancing over its surface, and it was radiating a great deal of power.

At this point, I heard a voice say, "The Earth is a green star of life." I realized then that what was radiating from this giant sphere wasn't exactly light or heat but vitality.

It was radiant with life.

This vision hovered before me for at least a couple of minutes, impressing itself upon me. Then the sphere sank back into the earth from which it had arisen.

Driving back home, I had the feeling that this vision was more than it seemed, that there was an important message for me here if I could figure it out. What did me being an avatar have to do with the earth as a "star of life?"

I suspect that whatever has been going on since that morning in the coffee shop, it's accelerating towards its denouement.

Or am I just thinking like a novelist, turning my life into a plot in one of my books?

I'd love to talk with the angel about this, but I suspect he'd disappear the moment the conversation got interesting.

I can't shake this feeling that something is about to break.

I just hope it isn't me!

Date ~ October 16

I haven't written for a week because my wife and I decided to go on a romantic getaway.

We rented a cabin in the mountains.

No computers.

No phones.

No television.

Just ourselves and the mountain.

I think the Mahaguru would be pleased.

Now, we're back, feeling recharged and renewed.

But I can't help but feel this week was the calm before the storm.

I was taking a nap in my study, lying down on my sofa, when the dream came.

At least, I thought it was a dream.

I was hovering in the air above a busy harbor. Great cargo ships were passing each other, some headed out to sea, others toward the dock. They were sleek vessels, unlike anything I recognized. They seem to be solar powered.

At the same time, in the sky over the harbor, a sleek airship was flying inland where I could see mountains in the distance. It looked like one of the zeppelins that flew in the years before the Second World War but again, with a sleek difference. Like the ships, I had the impression of a technology at work that was more advanced, yet in some ways simpler than our own.

In my dream, I flew over the city away from the harbor. The city was large but it was beautifully laid out. It seemed a network of neighborhoods connected by green spaces filled with trees and gardens. And the buildings, which were of varying height but no skyscrapers, were all curves and domes, with hardly any right angles in sight.

I had the impression, I don't know from what, that I was flying over a city in New Zealand but a very different New Zealand from the one I knew. The sea had risen, and coast lines around the world had changed.

Again, how I knew this, I don't know but dreams can be omniscient like that.

I flew to the outskirts of the city where I descended into a lovely garden. There, sitting on a bench, was a young man who apparently was waiting for me. I had no sooner landed then he got up and walked over to me. He was dressed in a one-piece outfit that covered him from his neck down to his ankles and wrists. It shimmered in the sunlight in a pleasing way that seemed functional rather than decorative, as if it were constantly monitoring and adapting to its environment.

He was an ordinary looking fellow, someone I might pass on the street and not notice. Except for his eyes. He had what I was now recognizing as the eyes of an avatar, shining with Light.

This is when things truly got strange.

I woke up, and he was there, standing by my sofa.

"Hello," he said, holding up one hand and shaping his fingers in a way that was different from but reminiscent of Spock with his Vulcan greeting. "I am Tomal." The accent was on the last syllable.

I reached out and touched him. He seemed perfectly solid.

"Are you real," I asked, scooting my legs over so he old sit down on the sofa, "or am I still dreaming?"

"You are not dreaming," he said, sitting himself gracefully next to me. "You were visiting my world, which is in your future. Now, I am visiting yours."

I was having a hard time wrapping my mind around this, even though I write science fiction, and time travel is one of the tropes.

"You're from my future?"

"I'm from the future that wants to be born."

"I don't understand. Are you a descendant of mine?"

"No, not genetically. But we are of the same Lineage."

"You mean, you're an avatar, too?"

He nodded. "I am what I am because of what you do as an avatar."

"You mean you became an avatar because of something I do?"

He smiled. "Yes. You make me possible."

This was too much, and I said so.

"Wait a minute! First, Sir Michael came and said that he had become an avatar due to something I did. Now you're saying you're an avatar due to something I will do. But for Heaven's sake, what is that? What did I do? What will I do?"

A flicker of doubt crossed his face. "Oh, dear!" he exclaimed. "You don't know?"

"Know what?" I shouted, exasperated.

He frowned. "I apologize. I misjudged the timing. I thought I was connecting with you after your realization."

"What realization?"

He stood up. "This is out of timing, and it's my fault. I must go. But if it's any consolation, I think it will come soon. I could not have been in error by more than a few hours or a day or so at most."

"What…what will be soon?"

But it was too late. He faded out and disappeared, the way they do in the Lineage, leaving me once again filled with questions and confusion.

And, I admit, a feeling of alarm.

Just what was coming?

I think the storm is breaking….

Nothing to report.

I still feel as if something is about to break. The air—or maybe it's just myself—feels supercharged.

I feel restless.

I have a headache.

Maybe I'm just coming down with the flu....

Last night, I had an amazing dream.

I dreamt I was in a large room that was divided into two halves by a wall of golden bars. Laying up against the side of the bars were rows of bouquets of flowers and colorful wreaths. Beyond, there were people going about their business. Occasionally, one of them would come out from the crowd, approach the bars, bow, and leave a bouquet as an offering.

I was on the other side of these golden bars, apparently a revered prisoner but a prisoner nonetheless.

Nor was I alone.

Lusanne, Sir Michael, the Mahaguru, and Tomal were on my side of the bars as well.

In fact, there were many of us behind these golden bars, the whole Lineage as far as I could tell.

And they were all looking at me, expectantly.

"What do you want me to do?" I asked.

"Set us free," Lusanne said.

"It's why you're here," chimed in Sir Michael.

"But how?" The bars looked very solid, and I couldn't see a door through them. As I looked about, two other people came up on the other side, bowed, and left flowers.

"Just remember," said the Mahaguru.

"Our future depends on it," Tomal said.

And I remembered.

I remembered why I was there, and as I did, the bars and flowers disappeared.

All of us walked out, then, and joined the multitude going about their ordinary affairs.

And I woke up.

Still remembering.

Today, I know who I am...and why.

The memories came.

I only hope I can find the words to write about it.

It turns out, I *am* an avatar but one whose job is to transform the meaning of being an avatar. To break down the golden bars of separation between being an avatar and being a person.

To take it out of the extraordinary and into the ordinary.

The sacredness of the ordinary.

I am the end of avatars!

And the beginning of "avataring."

Amazing!

It's two months ago today that I was having coffee in the coffee shop and suddenly remembered I was an avatar. Now the full memory has finally come.

I was working on my book in my study when I suddenly was someplace else.

Was I out of my body, astral traveling or something like that?

I don't know.

Maybe I simply fell asleep while working. I've done that before.

No matter. However it happened, I found myself in a small room, much like a monk's cell. But I wasn't in any monastery. I was in some kind of ancient temple. The walls were made of huge square blocks of stone, easily three feet or so on a side.

A door from the room led into a corridor lit by torches in sconces on the walls. The corridor walls, like those of the room I'd been in, were made from the same huge blocks of stone.

The whole place felt as if it had been ancient long before Atlantis or Lemuria fell into the waves.

I walked down the corridor until I came to a large room. It was empty except for a huge cube of stone in its center. If this was a temple, then this was the altar.

Rising at least six feet or so from the stone was a blue and silver flame. It gave off no heat, only a silvery light, but there was something immensely powerful about it. It was a living presence.

I thought of my angel in his Light form.

But this was a different order of magnitude.

I felt as if I were in the presence of a living star, anchoring itself in the bedrock of the earth.

I knew that this temple, if such it was, had existed since the Earth itself was born, though not in any physical way that we would understand. It *was* the bedrock of the Earth.

The silence in this room was profound and deep, a womb from which sounds had yet to be born. Yet, at the same time, the room was filled with an Intelligence, an ancient Knowing which flowed from the Flame into me.

And I Saw and Knew.

I saw the Earth, the green star I had seen in my vision that day in the forest, and I heard its calling to the cosmos for help in fulfilling its vision of being a "star of life."

It was like a piece of music but with an important chord missing.

It was an orchestra without all the necessary instruments for its symphony.

I saw this Flame coming in response, a Flame containing in itself a multitude of spirits, bringing with them Light and wisdom from experience in the Stellar Realms.

They were the missing chord.

They brought the missing instruments.

Science has always said our bodies are made from star-stuff. Now I could see our souls are, too. Made of the spiritual Light of stars.

These spirits blended with the star of the Earth, with Gaia, the World Soul, and from that union, human souls emerged and began their journey of evolution.

An evolution of the power to say yes to love and to make love part of the unfolding journey of life on Earth.

But evolution is a challenge, and being part of Earth

often meant forgetting our stellar and spiritual origins.

It meant forgetting to love, or even how to love.

Humanity "fell."

But even from the beginning, there were those who never forgot the love that was their source, or the power of their presence. They never forgot the music or their part in it.

They were those who remembered in the midst of life and sought to help others remember.

They became the avatars.

They became the Lineage of Remembrance and Service.

My Lineage.

But the reality is that all of humanity is the Lineage. We are all embodiments of the sacred, incarnations of love. We are all avatars, or as my son would say, representations of a greater identity playing the game of life.

We are not meant to be split between those who remember and those who do not, with the latter putting the former on pedestals…or on crosses.

We are all meant to remember.

We are all meant to be melodies and instruments of love.

And for this to happen, the thought-form of the avatar—the expectation that some unique, special individual will save us or lead us to a new world, that only one person can sing what must be sung or play what must be played—must be shattered. It must be transformed so we can all remember and see ourselves as avatars.

And that is the role I have taken.

To be the avatar that says that we don't need avatars because that is the identity we all have.

To be an avatar is to be fully human.

To be human is to be an avatar.

We are each an avatar, discovering our own sacred Way.

We can all turn *avatar* from a noun to a verb, "avataring" our way to bring love into the world.

To do this, I needed to lead an ordinary life, ignorant of being an avatar. Like Sir. Michael, I chose to forget who and what I was so I could have the experience of remembering. And when I remembered, I needed to work my way free of the thought-forms and expectations of what being an avatar meant or what I was "supposed" to do.

To come to the simple realization that we all have the power to love, a power of presence, and in that power, we are all avatars.

Nothing more is needed.

Tomal returned today, sitting on my sofa.

"This timing is better, isn't it? You have had your realization."

"Yes."

He smiled. "It is good. The small stone starts to roll, the avalanche will follow."

"You will be our future, then?"

"Nothing is guaranteed," he shrugged, "but the probability is more favorable. It will be slow. You will need kindness, courage, and compassion. Imagination, too. Humans do not wake up or change easily. But the process is underway."

"What must I do?"

"What you do best. Write! Put out the word. All humanity is the avatar."

He stood up. "You do not act alone now. Others will come forward to help. As I say, the avalanche begins. The one you knew as Senket…"

"My grandson now?"

"Yes. He comes to advance this unfolding and to add his wisdom and his spirit to what will now transpire." He began to fade out. "Remember, you are not alone. The Spirit of Humanity, past, present, and future, is your ally."

Then he disappeared.

I met with the Lineage today.

Where we were, I couldn't say. My body was asleep on the sofa in my study, but I was elsewhere.

A place of Light.

They were all there, many, many souls from all over the world, from every culture, every religion, every race, every gender. Some of them I knew, most of them I did not. There was Lusanne, the Mahaguru, Sir. Michael, even Tomal, who was an avatar because in his future, everyone knew they were an avatar. All of humanity had remembered and become the Lineage.

We met to say goodbye as avatars.

And hello to each other as human beings.

This is the call of the future: to be fully human.

It's how we survive the encounter with the elemental intelligences being invoked by our technologies.

It's how we find our true and proper place in the ecology of the world.

It's how we fulfill our ancient role, come in service to bring the power of love to Gaia, the Star of Life.

It's how we can be our Selves.

We are all the Lineage of Love.

The Human Lineage.

I now know who I am as an avatar.

An avatar of ordinariness.

An incarnation of the divinely ordinary.

Just like everyone else.

For we are all avatars, each of us in our way. Each of us is a sacred identity and presence.

We each have all we need to perform miracles: kindness, goodwill, cooperation.

We can listen to each other.

We can respect each other.

Mostly, we can love each other.

Everything else is icing on the cake, nice but not essential.

This time, I must have got it right, for my angel appeared.

This time, he was carrying a toy gold trumpet on which he gave me a celebratory, though off-key toot while somewhere faintly in the background, there were bells and whistles.

Angel humor.

Later, I was sitting on the porch, eating some toast. One of our crows landed nearby and strode over next to me.

He looked me in the eye and took a piece of toast from my hands. I knew he wasn't hungry.

It was a gift.

Love freely recognizing love.

I finally got it right.

I have much to do, now, so this may be my last entry.

Not as an avatar.

As a human person, helping people to remember.

I am, after all, a writer, and as Tomal suggested, I can spread these ideas through my books.

I can teach people to touch their Presence, their inner Light, and from that place to live their unique sacred way.

I can teach "avataring."

It's simple.

Choose joy.

Practice kindness.

Say yes to love.

Say yes to life.

Author's Note

Like all myths, this book is woven from non-fiction and fiction, the real and the imaginal, things that truly happened, and things that I made-up, all in service to a deeper truth. What parts are real? What parts invented? Does it matter?

May your heart know the truth.

David Spangler

David Spangler lives in the Northwest, is married and has four children. Since 1965, he has worked clairvoyantly and intuitively with a group of non-physical beings from the inner worlds of spirit. They identified themselves as being part of an inner school whose purpose was to explore and develop a spiritual teaching around the process of incarnation. This teaching is intended to empower incarnate persons living in the physical world — individuals such as you and me — to lead lives of greater blessing and capacity and to be sources of blessing and service for the world as a whole.

From 1970-1973, David was a co-director of the Findhorn Foundation Community in Northern Scotland. In 1974 he co-founded the Lorian Association, a non-profit spiritual educational organization, and continues to work with it today.

For further information on his work, voluminous writings and classes, please visit www.lorian.org.